A Book of Ritual Prayers

30 Celebrations for Parishes, Schools, and Faith Communities

Jerry Welte and Marlene Kemper Welte

Resource Publications, Inc.
San Jose, California

© 1998 Resource Publications, Inc. All rights reserved. No part of this book may be copied or reproduced without the permission of the publisher. For permission to reprint any part of this book, contact:

> Reprint Department
> Resource Publications, Inc.
> 160 E. Virginia Street #290
> San Jose, CA 95112-5876
> (408) 286-8505 (voice)
> (408) 287-8748 (fax)

Library of Congress Cataloging-in-Publication Data

Welte, Jerry, 1951–
   A book of ritual prayers : 30 celebrations for parishes, schools, and faith communities / Jerry and Marlene Kemper Welte.
       p.   cm.
   ISBN 0–89390–397–3 (pbk.)
   1. Worship programs.   2. Church year.   I. Welte, Marlene Kemper, 1949–   .   II. Title.
BV30.W43   1997
264—dc21   97-40488
                                                                             CIP

Printed in the United States of America.
02 01 00 99 98 | 5 4 3 2 1

Editorial director: Nick Wagner
Project manager: Mike Sagara
Cover design: Alan Villatuya
Production assistant: David Dunlap

Contents

Introduction 1

Advent/Christmas Celebrations

1. Celebrating Advent in Color:
   A Celebration of the Moods of God's Love 5
2. Shower God's People with Love:
   A Celebration of God's Graciousness 13
3. Dream of the Joyous Day to Come:
   A Celebration of Dreaming 17
4. Roses in December:
   A Celebration of Life from Death 25
5. On Angels' Wings: A Celebration of Presence 31
6. Shine Like Stars: A Celebration of Epiphany 41

Lent/Triduum/Easter Celebrations

7. The Ripple Effect: A Celebration of Connectedness 47
8. The Cross and the Flower: A Lent-Easter Celebration 55
9. Stone and Light: A Rite of Easter Witness 57
10. Come Sail Away: A Celebration of Being Lost and Found 65

Eucharistic Celebrations

11. Unless You Become a Child:
    An Adult Celebration of Childhood 77
12. Be the Light of Christ: A Family Rite for First Communion . . . 81
13. Gather Around God's Table:
    A Celebration of Community Re-membering 85

Reconciliation Celebrations

14. Let the Valleys Be Raised: An Advent Rite of Reconciliation . . 97
15. Building Bridges:
    A Family Celebration of First Reconciliation 101
16. Lighting the Way to Forgiveness:
    A Community Reconciliation Ritual 105

17. Digging in the Dirt, Washing in the Water:
    A Rite of Cleansing 109
18. Opening God's Gifts: An Advent Reconciliation Ritual 113

Opening and Closing Celebrations

19. Knock and the Door Will Be Opened:
    A Rite of Beginning 119
20. I Will Give You Rest: A Rite of Leavetaking or Closure 123
21. The Tree of Life: A Celebration of the Circle of Life 127
22. Building the House of God:
    A Celebration of Community Building 139

Miscellaneous Celebrations

23. Sharing the Seed of God's Blessings:
    A Celebration of Thanksgiving 153
24. Let Our Prayer Rise Before You:
    A Rite of Intercession 159
25. Many Yet One: A Celebration of Unity 161
26. Salt of the Earth: A Rite of Ecological Justice 163
27. Baptized in Water and the Spirit:
    A Prayer for Catechumens 167
28. I Will Plant a Seed: A Rite of Intercession 169
29. The Green and the Gold: A Rite of Balance 173
30. Home and Family Rites 177
    Cross 177
    Washing of Feet 178
    Oil 179
    Bread and Wine 179
    Word 180
    Laying On of Hands 181
    Fire 181
    Water 182

Introduction

Several years ago, in a Loyola course called "Sacraments and the Symbolic Life," Tad Guzie made a statement that has always stuck with us. He said that if you had asked an early Christian how many sacraments there are, the reply would have been something like: "Oh, I don't know, about a hundred and fifty." His point, of course, was that the early church did not think in terms of numbering sacraments but regarded all God's creation and countless human rituals as sacramental.

The rituals found in this resource are not intended to compete with, subjugate, or banalize the seven sacraments on which our church life is centered. These services are meant to be used with care, with pastoral sensitivity to the centrality of the Eucharist and the importance of the other sacraments. They should be implemented with a dignity and reverence that leads people back to the Eucharist rather than distracts them. The danger in the resources we provide lies in the temptation to use them as easy alternatives to continuing the challenging work of sacramental renewal. We hope that these services will be used responsibly.

That being said, let us immediately add that we have used every one of these rituals in parish or school settings. Each of them has been tested and refined and we have included only those which seemed to accomplish goals that are consistent with the spirit of the liturgical renewal.

We hope that you find the rituals included in this book to be "re-creational" experiences of reverent, participatory prayer. We hope that they engage your parish and school communities in prayer, stimulating their senses, intellects, and hearts. We hope, most of all, that they invite contact with the God of all creation and call people to be more responsible for that creation. It is our experience that using symbols as we do here does not reduce human awareness of the holiness of the sacraments but expands the church's appreciation of the sacramentality of all life and creation.

We have worked to make these services inclusive both in their language and rituals. While inclusivity leaves much room for flexibility and pastoral discernment, we hope that you will strive with us for this important value. We have listed authors and publishers of recommended prayers or musical resources as a guide to locating them. Where no author is listed, the work is original. The resources included here are intended to serve as broad outlines and suggestions that will be most effective when adapted to local pastoral circumstances and needs. We hope that you will do what is necessary on your part to make these rites work. This demands using the best materials possible, investing the necessary time to create a life-giving environment, and having the courage to let go of words so that these symbols and rites may speak for themselves. These resources have been developed in the long-standing church tradition of maintaining a rich liturgical life, full of a variety of rituals and devotions. This is the kind of experience that Andrew Greeley and Mary Durkin called for in their book *How to Save the Catholic Church*. We do not presume that these rituals will save the church, but we hope they will contribute to the church's constantly blossoming liturgical life.

Advent/Christmas Celebrations

1. Celebrating Advent in Color: A Celebration of the Moods of God's Love

This is more than an Advent service. It is an entire Advent program, a way of celebrating Advent. We first used it as a high school program for Advent, but it could be easily adapted for a parish or other faith community.

This program assigns a different color to each week of Advent and provides a way of celebrating each week of the season according to that color. Included here you will find: (1) an opening service to begin Advent; (2) a closing service to end Advent or to use just before Christmas break in an academic setting; (3) resources for each week of Advent to be used outside the liturgical services.

General Preparation

The main thing you need for the time outside the rituals is spools of colored ribbon in the four colors being used to celebrate the season. The four colors we used are below, but you may choose any four colors you wish. The ribbon is cut into six-inch lengths and distributed to the participants for wearing during the appropriate weeks. The color for week one is green; week two is blue; week three is red; and week four is white. The green and white ribbons will be distributed at the opening and closing liturgies respectively. The other ribbons can be given out at any convenient time near the beginning of the corresponding week.

Other resources listed below, such as readings, themes, qualities associated with each color, etc., can be used at your discretion. The main idea is to have the color for each week permeate the environment.

Colors of the Advent Wreath:
- green of the evergreen branches
- blue of the three candles (or violet if preferred)
- red of the ribbon
- white of the fourth candle (or Christmas candle)

Note: Our Advent rituals consistently suggest the use of blue colors rather than violet. We agree with those liturgists who find that using blue for Advent preserves the integrity of the season, reflecting a hopeful expectation that properly distinguishes Advent from the more penitential character commonly associated with the violet of Lent.

Week One: Green

Qualities: freshness/newness, hope, growth, renewal, fertility, adaptability

Focus:
- the earth/environment
- renewal of church & world
- hope for the oppressed
- women as new life for church
- resting in God (Ps 23)

Scriptures:
Jer 17:8 (He/she is like a tree planted beside the waters...its leaves stay green.)
Ps 23 (In green pastures God gives me rest.)
Gen 1:28–29 (See I give you every kind of green plant.)

Week Two: Blue

Qualities: tranquility, loyalty (true blue), depth (deep blue sea), surprise (out of the blue), sadness (the blues). Note: Similar color associations can be made by those using violet candles.

Focus:
- faithfulness/commitment
- sorrow/depression (holiday)
- depth/not shallowness (skin deep)
- stillness: patience/peace
- spontaneity

Scriptures:
Lk 2:8 (Shepherds kept watch at night; all is calm.)
Mk 4:35–41 (Jesus calms the storm at sea.)
Lk 2:51 (Mary pondered these things in her heart.)

Week Three: Red

Qualities: passion, strength, fire, excitement, life, action, warmth

Focus:
- just anger/anger as a virtue
- spirit, life, fire in our living
- taking action/getting involved
- compassion: feeling with others
- warming others amid life's cold

Scriptures:
Acts 2:2 (Pentecost: tongues of fire)
Mt 5:14–16 (You are the light of the world.)
Mk 11:15–18 (The Moneychangers)
Lk 12:49–51 (I have come to cast fire on the earth.)

Week Four: White

Qualities: awe, joy, light, purity, silence

Focus:
- keeping wonder alive/overcoming boredom
- time of silence/listen/communicate
- purity of heart: not perfection, but sincerity/single-heartedness
- being the light of the world
- being happy/lighten up/true joy

Scriptures:
Is 1:18 (Your sins will be made white as snow.)
Mt 17:1–8 (Transfiguration)
Mt 5:8 (Blessed are the pure of heart.)

Preparation for the Opening Ritual

- evergreen branches for the wreath or an evergreen wreath (not artificial)
- three blue candles for the wreath
- one white candle for the wreath
- a red ribbon for the wreath
- Dressing the dancers in the four colors for the service is effective. We made four simple pullover costumes, one in each color, for four dancers to wear.
- green ribbon cut into six-inch lengths (one for each participant)
- decorative baskets to hold the ribbons for distribution
- an aspergillium or a branch for sprinkling
- an undecorated Christmas tree (optional)

Outline for the Opening Ritual

- Gathering Hymn (any suitable Advent hymn)
- Signing in Faith/Sign of the Cross
- Opening Prayer (planner's/presider's option)
- Reading (Eccl 3:1–8: There is a season for every purpose.)
- Response (any sung setting of Ps 23: In green pastures God gives me rest.)
- Homily (sample reflection included below)
- Presentation/Blessing of The Advent Wreath (Choreograph presentation according to available dancers and space.)

1. Celebrating Advent in Color: A Celebration of the Moods of God's Love

Color/Leader	Action	Prayer (all respond)
Green dancer	presents wreath.	Color God's world with hope.
Blue dancer	presents candles.	Color God's world with peace.
Red dancer	presents ribbon.	Color God's world with love.
White dancer	presents candle.	Color God's world with joy.
Presider	sprinkles the wreath.	May it remain ever-green.
Youth reps	sprinkle the tree.	May it remain ever-green.
Dancers	distribute the ribbons.	(Hymn/music accompanies action.)
Adult reps	sprinkle the people.	May we remain ever-green.

- Sign of Peace
- Prayer (planner's/presider's option)
- Closing Hymn (any suitable Advent hymn)

Note: The following reflection is included here as a resource. Care should be taken, however, to tailor the reflection to your particular celebrating community. Consider, for example, the significance this service would take on in an inner-city parish where colors are gang trademarks and are often matters of life and death. Also, while we ascribe specific meanings to each color here, we minimized such explanations in our use of this service in order to maximize the ability of each participant to identify the meaning of each color symbol for him or herself.

Homily/Reflection

When we were children we found great happiness in the simple activity of coloring. At Christmas we received a new coloring book, pulled out a box of Crayolas, and colored away the hours to our heart's content.

How sad that growing up often means learning to put away our colors and look at the world as an adult, in black and white. Instead of seeing things in their many shades and hues, their combinations and contrasts, we are taught to divide the world into good and bad, right and wrong, winners and losers, haves and have-nots. The truth is that the world can never be so simple. When we try to make it so, it loses its beauty.

So today we begin our celebration of Advent by pulling out our colors again and pledging to see the world in color, to appreciate the rich and varied palette in which the world and its people are painted. We recognize that these colors live within us and will grow brighter or dimmer by the way that we live. Most of all, we proclaim that God can be born into the world in color and so the colors we wear actually reflect human hopes for God's colorful arrival.

We will wear blue and strive for the loyalty that is true blue, the clarity of a clear blue sky, the depth of a deep blue sea, the spontaneity that comes out of the blue, and the compassion that sings the blues with the lonely and abandoned.

We will wear red so as to live with spirit and fire, to fight angrily against the injustices which are heaped upon the poor, to remember those who have shed their blood in the cause of truth, and to blush in the realization of the great love which God shows us all.

We will wear white as a pledge to be lights for the world, to be pure in our intentions and desire, to wait in awe and silence for the miracle of God's coming, and to rejoice in a creation which reflects the glory of God in white clouds and white snow.

And today we begin by accepting these green ribbons to wear. We rejoice in green grass, green leaves, and green trees. We pray that the earth may be ever-green with life through our more responsible care for the earth. Finally, we take this green in order to be signs for a world in need of hope and new life.

1. Celebrating Advent in Color: A Celebration of the Moods of God's Love

Preparation for the Closing Ritual

- several rolls of white ribbon
- decorative baskets to hold the ribbons for distribution
- large vigil lamps (twelve inches) in the four colors of the season: green, blue, red, and white. These are available at any church goods store. The number of lamps depends on the size of the group and the worship space. You should have enough to create a strong four-color effect when the lights go down (we used twelve lamps of each color).
- Again, costumes for the dancers in the four colors are effective.
- If you have a selection of slides, set them to an instrumental version of "Silent Night" (a good one is on the CD *Mannheim Steamroller Christmas*).

1. As before, cut the white ribbon into lengths of about six inches and place them in the baskets for easy distribution.

2. Select representatives from each class or from the group to bear the candles in the assembly. Position them throughout the room and instruct them to keep their candles hidden until the Gospel, when the dancers will light them. Also instruct them about processing forward with the candles and placing them in designated areas, alternating the colors for maximum effect. You must determine the location and spacing of the candles that will achieve the best effect in your worship space. It is a good idea to practice this procession ahead of time.

3. Choreograph a dance for the presentation of the colors. We used long streamers in the four colors as well as one candle of each color.

Outline for the Closing Ritual

- Presentation of colors (In opening dance, each dancer bears one of the four colors; we choreographed the dance to "Coventry Carol," *Mannheim Steamroller Christmas.*)
- Gathering Hymn (any appropriate Advent hymn)
- Signing in Faith/Sign of the Cross
- Opening prayer

- Reading (Is 9:1–6)
- Response (Ps 27 setting "The Lord Is My Light," David Haas, GIA)
- Alleluia (sung as dancers light the candles that have been distributed in the assembly)
- Gospel (Jn 1:1–8 short form, lightbearers in the assembly are asked to hold their candles high during the Gospel.)
- Procession of candles (Lightbearers process and place candles in designated areas. The lights are dimmed so the colors dominate.)
- Hymn ("Silent Night" or other hymn, sung in the glow of the colored light)
- Slide reflection (We moved from the sung hymn to the instrumental recording of "Silent Night" for the accompaniment to the slides.)
- Distribution of Ribbons (Dancers move through assembly with white streamers while other dancers distribute white ribbons; participants are invited to wear these ribbons the rest of the day and throughout the Christmas season.)
- Hymn during Action ("The People That Walk in Darkness," Bob Dufford, New Dawn)
- Sign of Peace
- Recessional Hymn ("Joy to the World" or any joyful Advent/Christmas hymn)

2. Shower God's People with Love: A Celebration of God's Graciousness

This service allows participants to act out one of the most common Advent Scriptures (Is 45:8: Let the clouds rain down the just one). In doing so the participants come to a greater awareness of their personal responsibility to live its message. They realize that, like Jesus, they are God's love and justice poured out upon the world. It also employs the child-like winter activity of making snowflakes by cutting notches along several folds in a piece of white paper.

Preparation for the Ritual

- a large room with a high ceiling (We found a gym to be ideal.)
- a large box or boxes with flaps on the top and bottom
- a supply of cotton or fiberfill (quilt batting)
- glue (white or Elmer's glue works well)
- a long piece of wire or cord (used to raise and lower cloud)
- two other long pieces of cord (used to pull open the cloud from the ground)
- a pulley or hook on the ceiling of the room for the raising and lowering of the cloud
- enough pieces of white paper for each participant to make a snowflake (Recycle blank or nearly blank scrap paper if available.)
- The song "Shower the People," by James Taylor, makes an excellent slide reflection for this liturgy if you have appropriate slides (or the song can be used alone).

The instructions here presume that you are using one box (one cloud). If you want to use more than one cloud to maximize the effect or to accommodate a larger assembly, just repeat the instructions for each cloud.

1. Cut the short endflaps off the bottom and the top of the box so that only the longer sideflaps remain.

Advent/Christmas Celebrations

2. Glue the cotton or fiberfill to cover the outside of the box so that it looks like a cloud. Make the covering puffy rather than flat to better simulate the look of a cloud. You may find it necessary to support the fiberfill by tying white string or thread to the box in key areas.

3. Tie the long wire or cord securely to the top of the box, making sure that the box will hang balanced. Running the cord through the midpoint of both sides of the box and then tying it off in a triangle above the box works well.

4. Tie the two shorter cords to the two flaps on the bottom of the box, making sure the cords are long enough to be reached once the cloud is raised. The snowflakes will not weigh much, but you will need a piece of tape or other adhesive to hold the bottom flaps shut until you are ready to pull them open and release the snowflakes.

5. Arrange for the children or families involved to make their snowflakes ahead of time. They can be made at the liturgy, but time and cleanup factors make it more efficient for them to be made in class or at home ahead of time.

6. Test the cloud.

    a. Place some test snowflakes into the cloud.

    b. Run the long cord through the pulley/hook on the ceiling.

    c. Pull the free end of the cord to raise the cloud high and tie it off securely on a beam.

    d. Pull the two shorter cords to open the bottom flaps on the cloud and release the snowflakes.

    e. Make any adjustments that need to be made.

2. Shower God's People with Love: A Celebration of God's Graciousness

Outline for the Ritual

- Gathering Hymn ("O Come O Come, Emmanuel," traditional)
- Signing in Faith/Sign of the Cross
- Opening Prayer:
  > "Drop down dew, you heavens, from above and
  > let the clouds pour down the just one!"
  > Loving God, you sent Jesus down from the heavens
  > to plant justice for your people here on earth.
  > Send us forth also to pour out your love on the world.
  > May we be like the snow and rain
  > that constantly shower the people with divine love.
- 1st Reading (Is 45:8)
- Response (All come forward to place their snowflakes in the cloud. As participants offer their snowflakes, they show their willingness to be God's instruments in showering love and justice upon the world. When all snowflakes have been placed in the cloud it is raised.)
- 2nd Reading (Is 55:10–11)
- Gospel Acclamation
- Gospel (Lk 4:16–19)
- Homily/Reflection
- Ritual Action (Participants gather under the cloud(s); the cloud(s) is/are opened and the snowflakes drift down to shower God's children with God's love, an action which is realized in the symbols of ourselves.)
- Slide Reflection ("Shower the People," James Taylor)
- Blessing and/or Sign of Peace
- Dismissal
- Closing Hymn ("Sing Out Earth and Skies," Marty Haugen, GIA)

3. Dream of the Joyous Day to Come: A Celebration of Dreaming

This has proved to be a very effective ritual to "open up" Advent for its participants. We have used it in a high school setting, but it could easily be adapted for a parish community as an evening Advent service or part of an Advent week of prayer. It combines a ritual presentation and blessing of the Advent wreath with a reflection and prayer for the dreams of the community. The line in the title above, "Dream of the joyous day to come," is taken from the Christmas hymn "Still Still Still." The intention of the rite is to assist people in identifying and reaffirming their deepest and truest dreams for Christmas (what has been referred to as our "heart of hearts") in a culture that bombards us with advertising which suggests settling for lesser, materialistic dreams.

It is important for those who wish to use this service to call upon persons in your community with artistic skills and experience because the rite employs relatively simple but vital elements of drama and dance.

Preparation for the Ritual

For the Advent wreath presentation:

- enough evergreen branches to form a wreath when combined (These are available at nurseries or Christmas tree lots.)
- four candles for the wreath (as explained earlier, we prefer blue candles)
- a taper for lighting the wreath

For the dramatic presentation (in three parts):

- a recording of "Still Still Still" to play during the drama (We used Mannheim Steamroller's *A Fresh Aire Christmas*.)
- three or four dancers dressed in distinctive costumes to set them apart from the other players (The dancers represent or suggest an angelic presence.)
- a small Christmas tree decorated very simply (It should suggest what a poor family's tree might look like.)
- several boxes of different sizes and shapes wrapped in bright, colorful paper

- a person to play a child on Christmas morning
- a pair of pajamas (This is the costume for the child.)
- a table and chair (resembling kitchen furniture if possible)
- a 5" x 7" standing picture frame with a photo of a person in it
- a wall calendar
- a canvas bag or any traveling bag that suggests a person returning home for the holidays (Use a canvas bag if using scene II as described below.)
- two people (One plays the mother awaiting her son/daughter's homecoming; the other plays the person returning home.)
- a traveler's coat, hat, and gloves (Use a sailor's cap, blue coat, or fatigues if using scenario two as described below.)
- a park bench (or something that comes as close as possible)
- a newspaper
- a shopping bag and a few items to make it look somewhat full
- a comforter or blanket (one that looks warm and comfortable)
- someone to play a homeless or street person
- old, worn clothing to serve as a costume for a street person

For the dream reflection and prayer:
- an index card for each participant
- a pencil for each participant
- baskets to collect the cards
- a box with a lid, large enough to hold all the index cards
- Christmas wrapping to wrap the box and lid separately (lid must be removable)
- attractive Christmas ribbon to tie the box after the service

Setup for the Service

Place a covered stand or table in the area most central and visible to the assembly. This will be for the Advent wreath. The props described above should be placed behind the wreath and, if possible, should rest on a raised platform or step. The props should be set up as follows:

1. The decorated tree should be placed on the far right (stage right) with the wrapped boxes kept off to the side.
2. The table and chair should be placed in the middle.
3. The park bench should be placed on the far left with the newspaper resting on it.

Index cards and pencils may be handed to participants as they enter or may be placed in the pews/seats beforehand.

Play Summary:
Dreaming of the Joyous Day to Come

We will summarize the play here so that we can be more concise when we outline the service. It should be noted that any of the four scenes of the drama may be altered or replaced with a scenario of your choice. Scene II was included because we used this service during the Gulf War and several students had relatives serving in the Gulf. However, since the reuniting of family members for the holidays is such a universal experience, it would be a simple matter to delete the military aspect of the return and simulate the homecoming of any family member for the holidays. The entire play should take no more than about four or five minutes (the music we used ran about 3:40). There is no spoken dialogue, so it is important that the emotions be expressed through gesture and facial expression. This takes practice.

Scene I

The music begins. A child enters and moves toward the Christmas tree. She/he is running excitedly, hoping to find gifts for the opening on Christmas morning.

She/he suddenly stops and looks around; there are no presents. The space between the tree is barren. Saddened, she/he lays down next to the tree, falls asleep, and begins dreaming. In her/his dream, dancers move toward the tree with brightly colored packages and leave them beneath its branches. The dancers move off and a smile comes over her/his face as she/he continues sleeping.

Scene II

The music continues. A mother sits at a kitchen table. She picks up a picture frame that rests on the table and gazes at it longingly for it contains a photograph of her son/daughter who is away in the service. She stands and moves to a calendar on the wall. She flips the calendar a few months forward revealing a circled date, the date of her son/daughter's expected return. Sadly, she lets the calendar drop and returns to the table. She stares ahead momentarily, almost as if straining to see her son/daughter coming up the walk. She then sits down and puts her head down on the table. She falls asleep and begins dreaming. In her dream dancers escort her son/daughter into the room and move off. Her son/daughter places his/her bag on the table and gently shakes his/her mother. The mother does not awaken, so the son/daughter smiles and leaves his/her sailor's cap on the table, takes his/her bag, and moves off to unpack while the mother continues sleeping.

Scene III

The music continues. A homeless person enters and moves toward a park bench. Wearily she sits down on the bench and sets her bag beside her. She shivers from the cold and wraps her arms around herself seeking comfort. Spying the newspaper, she picks it up and opens it. She lays down on the bench and, as well as possible, covers herself with the newspapers. She falls into a restless sleep and begins to dream. In her dream dancers move toward her with a huge, warm comforter. They gently remove the newspaper and wrap her in the comforter. They dance off as the woman hugs the warmth around her and smiles in her continuing sleep.

Scene IV (Epilogue)

All three of the characters awaken from their sleep to find their dreams have come true. The child rejoices in her/his Christmas gifts; the mother finds the hat and hugs it to her; the homeless woman sits up and stares at the blanket around her in wonder. The lights go out and/or the players move off.

Outline for the Ritual

- Presentation of the 1st branch (The first evergreen branch is presented and laid on the table. This may be done by a member of the assembly or by a dancer. This branch begins the formation of the wreath and is accompanied by this prayer:)

3. Dream of the Joyous Day to Come: A Celebration of Dreaming

Prayer of the Evergreen

God of all life, we pray to be fashioned like the evergreen:
always new, always fresh, always green and alive.
The winter does not drain this branch of life;
its color is a sign that God is near.
May we too be ever-green at your coming.

- Presentation of Other Branches (The remaining branches are presented and laid in a circle while the following prayer is said:)

    Prayer of the Circle

    God without beginning or end,
    we pray to be reborn in this circle,
    a circle which includes all people as equals
    and makes a space within for God to be born.
    May we shape this sign in our hearts
    so that God may be born out of the circle of our lives.

- Presentation of Candles (The four candles are brought forth and set within the wreath in the appropriate places while the following prayer is said:)

    Prayer of the Blue

    God of all depth and wonder,
    our candles are blue and white.
    They hold the mystery of midnight
      and the promise of daybreak,
    our deepest sadness and our brightest hope.
    May we keep watch through the dark winter night for the dawn of your coming.

- Lighting of the Wreath (The first candle is lit while the following prayer is said:)

    Prayer of the Light

    God of all brightness,
    we present the first light of Advent:
    a small, single flame that will spread in the weeks ahead.
    May the light in our hearts grow also

to warm and brighten the world you love,
providing comfort and hope to those who wait.

- Gathering Hymn ("O Come O Come Emmanuel," traditional)
- 1st Reading (Jl 2:23; 3:1–3)
- Brief silence for reflection or sung responsorial psalm
- 2nd Reading (Phil 4:4–7)
- Dramatic Presentation (*Dreaming of the Joyous Day to Come*)
- Brief Homily (The homily we used is included below as a guide to shaping your own reflection for the people and time at hand.)
- Ritual Action (Each participant is invited to take one of the pencils and index cards provided and write down his/her deepest dream for Christmas. Dancers or other volunteers collect the cards in baskets and place them in the large, open wrapped box which is centrally located near the Advent wreath. When all the cards have been collected in the box, the wrapped lid is placed over it.)
- Blessing (The presider or minister may now say a simple prayer over the dreams and incense or sprinkle the box. The assembly may be invited to participate by extending their hands toward the box as the blessing is said.)
- Closing Hymn (any appropriate Advent hymn)

Note: After the service, the gift package containing all the community's dreams is sealed by tying it with Christmas ribbon. The box is then placed in a visible location in the community for the remainder of Advent so that all may continue to realize their dreams through prayer and reflection.

3. Dream of the Joyous Day to Come: A Celebration of Dreaming

Homily/Reflection

"I have a dream!"
So began Martin Luther King Jr.'s most famous words.
He believed enough in that dream to give his life for it.
Rosa Parks believed in the dream enough to risk stepping on
   that bus.
Christa McAuliffe also had a dream.
She gave everything for one flight;
the dream meant that much to her.
Advent is a time for dreaming.
From the time we are small we are taught to answer one question:
"What do you want for Christmas?"
But we must grow up and so must our dreams.
My son told me he dreamed he got a new car for Christmas.
I told him to go back to sleep and try again.
Advertising teaches us to continue dreaming like a child.
"I own my own mink" one woman proudly announces;
but the world needs better dreams than that.
Today we want to take some time for dreaming,
But we want to identify our deepest, truest dreams,
those that come from our heart of hearts.
What do you really want for Christmas?
What is your dream for your life, your family, your world,
   your church?
These dreams will be our gifts to one another;
Each of you is asked to make your wish and write it down.
These dreams will be collected and sealed in a package
to be placed outside the ministry office during Advent,
so that we all may remember our dreams and pray for them.
So take a few moments and choose your dream.
Then take the card, and write it down, then place it in the basket.
Then each time you pass by the ministry office during Advent,
remember your dream and the dreams of those gathered here.
Pray that our dreams may come true this Christmas season.

4. Roses in December: A Celebration of Life from Death

This is a set of two rituals that are ideal for opening and closing an entire Advent program. The first service is to be celebrated in the first week of Advent; the second during the fourth week. We do not recommend using these rites in the context of the Eucharist. These services provide a symbol which serves as an effective focus for the Advent season as well as an invitation to action through almsgiving, which allows people to remain aware of the poor during a time when the culture is encouraging narcissistic consumerism. We celebrated these rituals on a huge scale with two thousand high school students and an extensive environmental setup. Some of the descriptions below may reflect that scale and sound intimidating. The setup and execution of these rites, however, is easily adaptable to smaller groups and simpler environments, to parish as well as educational settings.

The focal point for this Advent program is the symbol of the rose, an important and recurring symbol in the Advent Scriptures ("Let the earth open and salvation bud forth" [Is 45:8]), in Christian tradition (Our Lady of Guadalupe), as well as in popular culture (Bette Midler's "The Rose"). Since we developed these rites at an all-girl's high school, we were also inspired by the story of Jean Donovan's martyrdom in El Salvador. The title for this set of rituals is taken from her words and is also the title of an excellent videotape on her life, which we recommend offering as part of this Advent program. The symbol of the rose in December, of course, simply offers a variation on the paschal mystery theme, but we found it to be a particularly beautiful and effective one.

General Preparation

- an advent wreath (large enough to remain prominent in environment)
- an open space upon which to set up a "snowscape" environment
- enough quilt batting to cover the selected space with "snow" (This comes in rolls and is available at fabric stores.)
- a quantity of seed, enough for each participant to sprinkle a pinch of it in the snow (Thistle seed works well.)
- glass dishes or bowls in which to place the seed for planting

- small artificial roses with wire stems, one for each participant (These are available at craft or fabric stores, but large amounts may require you to special order early.)
- a supply of toothpicks, one for each rose
- a supply of small banks, one for each participant or family (Plastic cups with lids work well and can be obtained in bulk at outlet or wholesale stores.)
- a supply of labels to mark each bank with "Roses in December." Computer labels work well, print fast, and are easy to apply.
- a recording of "Love Changes Everything" from Andrew Lloyd Webber's *Aspects of Love*
- a collection of slides including shots of roses (optional)

Optional items listed below can enhance the effect of the snowscape depending upon how extensive an environment you wish to create, taking into account time, space, and budget.

- a round mirror to simulate an ice pond
- pine cones
- artificial white twigs (sold at most craft stores)
- glitter to create a sparkling effect when sparingly sprinkled upon quilt batting
- white artificial snowflakes to scatter over the quilt batting
- two or three evergreen trees, natural or artificial, to set up on the snowscape
- bags of fiberfill to place around the mirror, the tree bases, and other key areas to disguise any artificial aspects of the setting

Preparation for the Opening Ritual

1. Set up your snowscape. You must determine its size, location, and cost. Ours covered the entire width of an auditorium stage. That made it impressive to look at but rather expensive and a lot of work to put up. Also consider whether you can leave the environment in place during Advent. After deciding these specifics, begin the work of rolling out the quilt batting and adding whatever extra touches

you have chosen. If you are looking for a model for the setup, we found it helpful to visit a Christmas supply store. Many of them create similar snow scenes in order to showcase their merchandise. We got several good ideas from looking at such displays.

2. Prepare your Advent wreath and display it in a place of prominence. The wreath should remain a focal point of the liturgy and not be compromised by the snowscape. We placed the wreath in the midst of the assembly to set it apart and had the first lighted candle solemnly carried in to the wreath in darkness.

3. Prepare your banks. These are given out to each person/family at the opening service. The idea is for them to take the bank home and save money for some chosen cause or group during Advent. The banks are returned at the closing service with whatever contributions have been saved. We made computer labels printed with "Roses in December" and applied one to each bank. You should plan to have people assist with the distribution of the banks at the liturgy. Finally, and most important, you must choose which group or cause the contributions will support. We contributed our collection to Mary's Pence. The name of the group being supported can be printed on the label for each bank.

4. Four or five of the glass bowls or dishes should be spaced along the front of the snowscape and filled with thistle seed.

Outline for the Opening Ritual

- Lighting of Advent Wreath (according to local custom or preference)
- Gathering Hymn ("O Come O Come Emmanuel," traditional)
- Signing in Faith/Sign of the Cross
- Opening Prayer (from Advent prayers in sacramentary or original)
- 1st Reading (Is 45:8 [More verses may be used if desired.])
- Response ("Patience People," John Foley, New Dawn)
- 2nd Reading (2 Cor 9:6–11)
- Gospel Acclamation
- Gospel (Mk 4:26–29)

- Reflection/Homily (Roses in December/explanation of the banks)
- Ritual Action: Planting of Seeds/Receiving of Banks (Members of the assembly process forward and approach the snow field. Each participant takes a small pinch of seed and "plants" it in the snow. Each individual/family then receives a bank to keep during the Advent season in which to make contributions to the identified cause or group.)
- Hymn ("Lo How A Rose E'er Blooming" sung by choir during action)
- Advent Litany (All respond to invocations; not all invocations need to be used.)

    Response: Come, Lord Jesus.

    Leader:
    - There is cold penetrating the warmth of our cities... *(Response)*
    - There is loneliness shadowing the light in our hearts... *(Response)*
    - There is hunger hardening the ground of our hope... *(Response)*
    - There is anger choking off the roots of peace... *(Response)*
    - We have been given seeds of life... *(Response)*
    - We have been given the warmth of love... *(Response)*
    - We have been given a surplus of food... *(Response)*
    - We have been given the spirit of peace... *(Response)*
    - Flowers still bloom amid the coldest winter... *(Response)*
    - Life still grows beneath the deepest snow... *(Response)*
    - Beauty still breaks through the hardest ground... *(Response)*
    - Peace still blossoms amid the storms of war... *(Response)*
    - May the seed we plant grow from within... *(Response)*
    - May the love we seek spring forth in our hearts... *(Response)*
    - May the rose we await bloom in our spirits... *(Response)*
    - May the life we create take root in our God... *(Response)*
- Sign of Peace

4. Roses in December: A Celebration of Life from Death

- Blessing
- Closing Hymn ("Song of All Seed," text by Huub Oosterhuis, OCP)

Preparation for the Closing Ritual

1. Whether you are reassembling the snowscape for the closing or not, remove all the seeds from the surface of the snow. We found the easiest way to do this was to pick up the roll of quilt batting, shake it out, and then put it back in place.

2. The roses must be "planted." We accomplished this by wrapping the wire stem of each rose around a toothpick and then sticking the toothpick into the quilt batting. We found this to be hard work, so either get a lot of help or find a method that works better for you. Spread the roses out for maximum effect.

3. Again, place your advent wreath in a central location.

4. Depending on how much money you are expecting from the collection, you may want to place baskets or boxes around the front of the worship space so that people can place their contributions in them as they process forward. Banks may be collected as the procession moves by or you may ask the people to dispose of their own banks.

5. If you have someone with experience putting slides to music for a reflection, have that person prepare your available slides to the music of "Love Changes Everything." If no slides are available, you may still find a way to use the song in some other manner.

Outline for the Closing Ritual

- Lighting of Advent Wreath accompanied by "Lo How A Rose E'er Blooming" from the *Narada Christmas Collection, Volume 2*
- Gathering Hymn (any appropriate advent hymn)
- Signing in Faith/Sign of the Cross
- Opening Prayer:

    Creator God, giver of the rose,
    the source of beauty, the promise of peace;
    the renewal of love, the herald of life;
    flower again in our lives today.

Bloom in us with the power of the rose.
Come with its promise of hope to the world.
We ask this in the name of Emmanuel,
who is "God with us." Amen.

- 1st Reading (Is 61:1–2,10–11)
- Response ("God Is Love," David Haas, GIA)
- 2nd Reading (1 Thes 5:16–24)
- Gospel Acclamation
- Gospel (Mt 1:18–25)
- Homily (We used the song "Love Changes Everything" as an inspiration for the homily.)
- Ritual Action: Offering of Contributions/Picking of Roses (Members of the assembly are invited to process forward. Each one offers whatever money has been collected in the bank and picks one of the roses that now grows out of the snow where the seeds were planted.)
- Slide Reflection ("Love Changes Everything")
- Hymn ("Silent Night," traditional, or other suitable Advent/Christmas hymn)
- Sign of Peace/Dismissal Rites
- Closing Hymn (any appropriate hymn of your choice)

5. On Angels' Wings: A Celebration of Presence

Here we present a means of celebrating the entire season of Advent rather than an individual rite. The rituals included form the opening and closing to a fully developed observance of the season. As outlined, this approach is ideal for academic or religious education settings, but it could easily be adapted for a parish or community observance of the Advent season. The simplest way of understanding this approach to Advent is to see it as the angelic version of the Kriss Kringle tradition. Participants choose the name of one other individual and are invited to be that person's "Advent angel" throughout the season. In a context of prayer the community invites its members to respond creatively to our common call to realize God's presence in the life of each person. This may be done in any number of ways, including prayer, notes, simple gifts, kind words, etc. True to the spirit of God's messengers, all angels remain anonymous or "invisible" while performing these acts of kindness. Angel identities may be revealed at the end of the season at your discretion.

The opening ritual is built around the choosing of names, while the closing celebration culminates with all the angelic participants "receiving their wings" a la Clarence in *It's a Wonderful Life*. During the season, classrooms or volunteer groups cut out and decorate the angel wings that will be presented at the closing celebration, even as everyone continues their angelic deeds. It all sounds rather corny, but it works! It is one of the best approaches we have found for keeping Advent as a season while maintaining the community's focus on what that season is about: announcing the Good News, doing for others, reincarnating God's presence in the world.

The "arts and crafts" component of this observance may suggest that it be used on the grade school level, but we first developed this in a high school setting and found that it generated a high level of enthusiastic participation. The year after we used this approach a number of students asked why we weren't doing it again. Ironically, our development of these services coincided with the beginnings of a significant cultural interest in angels. While we would love to indulge the fantasy of having such immediate impact on the culture, we humbly decline credit for this phenomenon.

General Preparation

For the Opening Service

- an advent wreath
- a large symbol or representation of an angel (optional)
- the name of each participant printed on an individual card or slip of paper
- a basket or baskets from which the names will be drawn (The number of baskets depends on the size of the assembly.)
- a recording of "No One Is Alone" from Stephen Sondheim's musical *Into the Woods*

For Making and Decorating the Angel Wings:

- a stencil or outline for your angel wings about two inches high by four inches wide (We suggest having an artist in your community draw the wings, or you can trace an outline from the many picture resources available in season.)
- a way of reproducing and cutting out the angel wings (We recommend putting several wing outlines on one master sheet which you can photocopy onto card stock to give wings weight and durability.)
- supplies for decorating the wings (markers, glitter, glue, etc.)
- a hole punch for putting a small hole at the top center of each set of wings
- ornament hooks, one for each set of wings

For the Closing Service

- a long piece of white quilt batting large enough to form a "cloud" backdrop upon which to hang all the wings you have created (This is found at craft or fabric stores.)
- a manger scene proportional in scale to your worship space and the size of your quilt batting backdrop

5. On Angels' Wings: A Celebration of Presence

Preparation for the Opening Ritual

1. Print or type the name of every participant on individual cards or labels (computer label printouts are ideal if you have a database containing all the names of those participating). Make sure that no one is left out!

2. Place the names in baskets for distribution and drawing of names during the service. Use enough baskets so that the drawing of names will not take unduly long. Place the baskets so that they are readily visible to the assembly.

3. Place a large symbol or representation of an angel at a prominent place in your environment (optional). We displayed a large stained glass angel that we had made for a previous Advent service (made with foam board and colored plastic gel or cellophane).

4. Place your Advent wreath in a prominent position (the angel should not overshadow the wreath). We suspended the stained glass angel over the Advent wreath.

5. If you are using a dialogue reading of the annunciation, assign lectors to their respective parts. Those with access to a drama department may choose to have Mary or the angel dress the part.

6. If you are including a dance or gestured prayer to "No One Is Alone," assign the necessary ministers of dance to prepare choreography and practice.

Outline for the Opening Ritual (1st Week of Advent)

- Gathering Hymn ("O Come O Come Emmanuel," traditional)
- Lighting of the Advent Wreath (local custom or preference)
- Signing in Faith/Sign of the Cross
- Opening Prayer:

    Emmanuel, God with us,
    once again your world watches, waits, and wonders:
    Where have you gone? When are you coming?

    As in times past when your people looked to the
    mountains for the messenger of peace to appear,
    so do we long for the arrival of your messengers
    of peace, and protection, and presence.

    Once again, as in Advent days of old,
    send your angels to brighten the darkness,
    to warm the cold, to fill the silence.

    May we too be your messengers of hope,
    your songs of gladness, your fire of love,
    so that you may be born again in this time and place,
    Emmanuel, God with us.

- 1st Reading (Is 52:7–10,12)
- Response (Ps 91; setting: "Be with Me Lord," Marty Haugen, GIA)
- 2nd Reading (Eph 4:30–5:2)
- Gospel Acclamation
- Gospel (Lk 1:26–38 [See note below for dialogue format.])
- Homily (See below for "Parable of the Guardian Parents.")
- Dance Prayer (gesture or dance prayer to "You Are Not Alone" [optional])
- Ritual Action: Drawing of Names (The baskets are passed; each participant draws the name of one member of the community and

becomes that person's anonymous "Advent angel" for the entire season.)

- Instrumental Music/Hymn (played to accompany ritual action)
- Sign of Peace
- Closing Prayer/Blessing (your choice)
- Closing Hymn ("How Beautiful," Joe Wise [PAA])

Note: When we developed a dramatized version of the annunciation, we incorporated inclusive language into it along with some other minor changes. The assembly can play the role of the angel while one woman/girl plays the part of Mary, or the assembly can take the part of Mary while one person assumes the role of the angel. Those working with teens should be aware of the issue of teenage sex when making choices regarding roles and text (e.g., dropping the second half of the line: "How shall this happen, because I am a virgin?").

Homily: Parable of the Guardian Parents

Our homily emphasized how Advent calls us to embody God's presence for others rather than to passively wait for God to arrive. The parable below suggests that God has placed us in each other's hands and so may be voiceless or "paralyzed" without us. It is included here as an optional resource.

The story is told of a woman named Angela who grew up under the care of a strong and loving couple. Her mother and father were always there for her, protecting her from danger, guiding her in troubled times, and always showing their love for her. Even as a child Angela realized how special her parents were and often told them of her gratitude and affection.

On the day of her twenty-first birthday Angela's parents asked to speak with her. "We have something important to tell you," they said. Gently they explained that they were not her real parents, that her true parents had entrusted her to them when she was just an infant.

Angela was so stunned she could not speak, but then she demanded to know why her parents had abandoned her. "We made a promise not to tell you that," her foster parents said. "We can only assure you that your parents love you very much."

Angela could not begin to accept their explanation. What kind of parents could abandon their own child to strangers and still claim to love her? From that day on she dedicated herself to finding her true parents and confronting them. Her confusion and hurt grew as she searched records and traced the trail of her life back to her childhood, where she discovered who her parents were and where they lived. Her anger was at a peak as she banged on the front door of her lost parents' home.

A young woman who looked like a nurse answered the door. Immediately Angela explained who she was and announced her determination to see her parents. The woman hesitated, but then she opened the door and motioned for Angela to follow her. They came to a room upstairs which the nurse entered alone for a moment. When she came out she motioned Angela into the room saying: "Your parents will see you now."

When Angela entered the room her eyes widened and she hesitated. Inside were a man in a wheelchair and a woman in a bed. The man wheeled forward but did not speak. "Are you my parents?" Angela asked. The man still did not speak but only nodded slowly. "Why didn't you take care of me?" Angela insisted. "Why did you give me up?" The man finally picked up a small tablet, wrote on it, and handed it to her: "I cannot speak, and your mother cannot move. She is paralyzed." He then gave Angela a letter that had obviously been written some time ago. It explained how her parents had suffered their injuries in an auto accident just after she was born and had decided they could not take care of her properly. They searched long and hard until they found the two people who they knew would give her all the love they had in their hearts but could not express with their broken bodies. Angela walked to her mother lying on the bed and saw tears welling up in her eyes. "I love you," was all her mother could say.

5. On Angels' Wings: A Celebration of Presence

Preparation for the Closing Ritual

1. Obtain the wing stencil or outline and reproduce it on card stock of a desired texture and weight (paper heavier than 20 lb. bond).

2. Cut out and decorate the wings. Encourage creativity, variety, and artistry. We found it simpler and neater to decorate an entire sheet of wings before cutting them out.

3. With a hole punch or the tip of a math compass place a small hole in each of the decorated wings at the center near the top.

4. Insert an ornament hook in each set of wings so that the hook faces the back or undecorated side of the wings.

5. Roll the length of quilt batting out flat against a wall or other support structure and fix it in place with tape or other means (the size of the batting is proportional to your worship space and number of wings).

6. Hang the wings by pushing the hook into the quilt batting (arrange and space the wings attractively on the batting).

7. Set up the Advent wreath, angel (if available), lectern, etc. We also used a few poinsettia plants to enhance the environment.

Outline for the Closing Ritual (4th Week of Advent)

- Lighting of the Advent Wreath (according to custom or preference)
- Gathering Hymn ("Let the Valleys Be Raised," Dan Schutte, New Dawn)
- Signing in Faith/Sign of the Cross
- Opening Prayer:

    > The angels appear! The light of glory dawns,
    > and the bright promise of morning wakes.
    > The song of peace is heard,
    > and every heart knows the story of love is true.
    > The comfort of presence is felt,
    > and hope lives on because God is near.
    > In this season, O loving God,
    > let every heart know your love;
    > let every land embrace your peace;
    > let every child feel your joy.
    > May we pledge ourselves throughout this season
    > to be messengers of your arrival,
    > to herald the news of your coming:
    > The world is good! Life has meaning! No one is alone!
    > We join the choirs of angels in this song of hope,
    > for you are Emmanuel, God with us!

- 1st Reading (Ps 91; we felt this text merited the exception of using a psalm as a reading; it could also be used in antiphonal form as an opening prayer.)
- Response (Ps 139; setting: "You Are Near," Dan Schutte, New Dawn)
- 2nd Reading (1 Jn 4:7–12)
- Gospel Acclamation
- Gospel (Lk 2:1–14)
- Homily (See "Parable of the Angel's Wings" below.)

- Ritual Action (Having earned their wings by embodying the presence of God, the members of the assembly process forward, select a set of angel wings from the cloud backdrop, and return to their seats. Another option is for community representatives to present the wings.)
- Slide Reflection (optional; during Advent we took slides of the community engaged in various charitable works and showed them at the service with a background of instrumental music.)
- Sign of Peace
- Blessing
- Closing Hymn ("Go Tell It on the Mountain, " traditional)

Homily: Parable of the Angel's Wings

We wrote this parable as a companion piece for this service. We wanted the homily to emphasize what forms the essence of being a messenger of God. It is not the honor of having wings but the spirit of love in one's heart. As before, we include the story here as a resource for you to use at your discretion.

>There was once an apprentice angel named Samantha who longed more than anything to receive her wings and fly. The time of her apprenticeship was difficult because she was impatient to be past all the training and to know the joy and freedom of flight that she had seen so many other angels achieve. The truth was that the logic behind the entire process of earning one's wings was a mystery to her. In her mind she knew that she was more deserving of flight than many of the angels who had already been awarded their wings. Just yesterday Samantha had been talking with some friends about Marissa, the latest addition to the company of angels. Samantha and her friends felt that Marissa was the least deserving of apprentices and they couldn't understand how she could have been awarded wings ahead of them. They laughed at the thought of Marissa in flight, so ugly and awkward. They would certainly make more graceful use of those wings than she.
>
>As time went by Samantha's impatience grew. She did not understand why she had not been awarded her wings. Unable to

wait any longer, she decided to take matters into her own hands. One night she slipped into Marissa's room and stole her wings. She was confident that she could prove her superiority over Marissa and earn the right to keep the wings she was taking. Samantha put on the wings and hurried to a place where she could test them. Full of anticipation, she leaped into the air and was shocked when instead of soaring above the clouds she fell heavily to the ground. Shaken, but still determined, she adjusted the wings and again launched herself skyward. Again, however, she only crashed to the ground with a thud. She heard a voice call her name and turned to see Grace, the leader of the angels, watching her with a smile.

"These wings are defective," complained Samantha. "They don't work." "There is nothing wrong with the wings," replied Grace. "It is not the wings of an angel that give flight; it is the heart. You cannot fly because your spirit is still heavy with anger and pride. When you learn to love and to give, your heart becomes light and full of joy, and you will take flight like the other angels. Only then will you earn your wings, the sign of a free and caring heart." Samantha was about to protest when she caught a glimpse of something above her. She looked up and saw Marissa, missing the wings that Samantha had taken, soaring through the clouds like a bird.

6. Shine Like Stars: A Celebration of Epiphany

This ritual uses the Christmas story of the magi to celebrate the call to be "the light of the world" in a particular way. As the service begins a stable stands in a prominent area. Behind the stable is a large, dark blue backdrop, representing the empty night sky. Each participant comes to the celebration with a bright yellow star cut out of cardboard, or stars can be provided as participants arrive. Each star has some sort of fastener on the back (doubled masking tape, safety pin, Velcro, etc.) so that it can be attached to the sky. After the readings and the homily the backdrop will be lowered and the participants will process forward and offer their stars to fill up the empty sky, committing themselves to lighting the way to Jesus, to lead people to the presence of Christ by the way they live. Once all have offered their light, the backdrop will be raised and Christ will be more visible in the world. We have found that this service works especially well with those of grade school age and their families.

Preparation for the Ritual

- a large piece of deep blue material, or several smaller pieces that can be sewn together (If you are using tape to fasten the stars, make sure your material will hold it. The size of the fabric is flexible to your circumstances, but we have found that the bigger, the better. The piece we have used measures about ten feet high and twenty feet wide. The remnant tables at fabric stores are good places to look for material.)

- a cardboard star for each participant (These can be easily cut out of yellow poster board. We made each star four inches high. Make sure to use the four-pointed star of David rather than the usual five-pointed star.)

- adhesive tape or pins for each star

- two long lengths of cord or wire to use for raising and lowering the cloth (If the cloth sags in the middle it may be necessary to support the middle with a third cord; otherwise, some of the stars may fall off as the cloth moves.)

- hooks or pulleys that can be mounted high on the wall to run the cords through
- a stable with figures to place in front of the sky

Note: It is important when raising the cloth to have people on both sides to guide it gently upward as it is raised. Rough or uneven movement might dislodge stars and minimize the beauty of the sign. We have found that when this sign is celebrated well it elicits delightful responses from the assembly, especially from young children.

Suggested Outline for the Service

- Gathering Hymn ("We Three Kings" or other Epiphany hymn)
- Signing in Faith/Sign of the Cross
- Opening Prayer (from the feast of Epiphany)
- 1st Reading (Is 60:1–3)
- Response (Ps 27; setting: "The Lord Is My Saving Light," Andrew Witchger, GIA)
- 2nd Reading (Phil 2:14–16)
- Gospel Acclamation
- Gospel (Mt 2:1–11, the story of the magi)
- Homily (A possible focus could be the contrast between our culture's preoccupation with "being a star" or famous and the Christian notion of being a star or light.)
- Ritual Action (Each participant processes forward and attaches a star to the night sky, so offering to be a light drawing others to the presence of Christ.)
- Litany of Light:

    Response: Arise! Let your light shine for all to see.

    Leader:
    - For those lost in selfishness... *(Response)*
    - For those lost in loneliness... *(Response)*
    - For those lost in hatred... *(Response)*

6. Shine like Stars: A Celebration of Epiphany

- For those lost in darkness... *(Response)*
- You are a sign that love is stronger than hate... *(Response)*
- You are a sign that love heals loneliness... *(Response)*
- You are a sign that love unites those divided... *(Response)*
- You are a sign that love lights up the darkness... *(Response)*
- Many find little reason for hope and joy... *(Response)*
- Many see only darkness and gloom ahead... *(Response)*
- Many are in search of God... *(Response)*
- Many wise people still follow Christ's star... *(Response)*
- Blessing
- Dismissal
- Closing Hymn ("We Are the Light of the World," Jean A. Greif, Vernacular Hymns)

Lent/Triduum/Easter Celebrations

7. The Ripple Effect: A Celebration of Connectedness

The two rituals we titled "The Ripple Effect" celebrate exactly what they suggest: we are connected to each other and to creation; each of our actions affects the living things around us for good or for ill. Using pools of water and stones, two powerful Christian symbols, we involved the assembly in this cosmic mystery. This pair of rituals is ideal for opening and closing Lent while providing a focus for the entire season that can serve as a context for follow-up adult education, youth programs, or service projects. It even ties in nicely with the Rite of Christian Initiation of Adults because it signifies our interconnectedness, how we influence one another through faith and action. We first celebrated these rites in a high school setting and found "The Ripple Effect" to be an effective countercultural sign in a society of pervasive individualism. The mystical quality of the service tends to make its truth creative and life-giving rather than academic or preachy.

Because of high school scheduling constraints we celebrated the opening rite on Ash Wednesday. While this approach allowed us to "open" the season of Lent in an integral fashion, it may not be the ideal if the day's central symbol of ashes is eclipsed by "The Ripple Effect." Although the outline below will describe the opening rite as part of an Ash Wednesday service, you may want to consider offering it as part of an early Lenten evening of prayer or parish mission. For the same reason, the closing service outlined later "anticipated" Easter a bit for pastoral reasons we explain below. We recommend that parishes adapt this service to maintain a Lenten flavor and celebrate it during the Fifth week of Lent to avoid cluttering Holy Week. We realize that schools and religious education programs may need to make pastoral decisions that affect the shape of their liturgies; we only ask that such decisions be made with sensitivity to the integrity of the liturgy and be in harmony with your particular parish's liturgical life.

General Preparation

- ashes (if celebrating on Ash Wednesday)
- a large round pool (We suggest a solid blue pool or one that can be "disguised" to look like a pond rather than a toy. A round pool facilitates the rippling of the waters.)

- a garden hose to fill the pool once set up indoors, unless the idea of a bucket brigade appeals to you (Most utility sink faucets have threading for a hose.)

- several plants or small trees to place around the pool to disguise its artificial look and create a natural environment (We rented some small trees from a nursery, but if you plan to leave the environment in place during Lent, this could be very expensive.)

- several "mini pools" for the closing service only (Twenty-inch plastic "terra pot" saucers are ideal and are available in many craft stores and nurseries. Each participant will drop a stone into a saucer, so obtain enough to facilitate the procession and the distribution of stones. Too many stones in one saucer impedes the ripple effect.)

- a paschal candle for closing liturgy in a school (See rationale.)

- a narrator and actors/dancers to act/dance "The Parable of the Two Stones" (optional)

- a supply of small dark stones and small light stones, enough for each participant to have one of each (We used white landscaping marble for the light stones and black obsidian for the dark. You may opt for a supply of landscaping stones of one color and type, enough for each participant to have one stone.)

Note: We used black and white stones because of their many symbolic connections, both spiritual and psychological (Jungian), to the tension between good and evil, light and shadow. Yet, our concern in doing this was the danger of suggesting racial stereotypes: "white is good and black is evil." We minimized this problem by referring to the stones as "dark and light" rather than "black and white." Also, when talking about the ripple effect, we avoided specifically associating the white stone with good and the black stone with evil; instead, we referred to the stones and their effects as "opposites." This allowed our black students the freedom to identify the dark stone as their positive side and the white stone as their "shadow" (see "The Parable of the Two Stones" below). If you fear this problem cannot be overcome by such adjustments, it is easy to adapt by choosing different colors or by obtaining only one kind of stone and giving each participant only one stone to carry during Lent. The parable, however, is difficult to use without the tension between the two types of stones.

7. The Ripple Effect: A Celebration of Connectedness

Preparation for the Opening Ritual (Presuming an Ash Wednesday Service)

1. Make whatever arrangements and setup you have planned for the blessing and distribution of ashes.
2. Choose a place to set up the pool. Surround it with the plants and whatever other environmental touches you wish to include. Do not obscure the assembly's direct view of the pond because this is essential for the parable and the overall effect.
3. Display the stones in baskets or other containers so that they are visible to the assembly and accessible for distribution.
4. Connect the hose and fill the pool to a suitable level.

Outline for the Opening Ritual (on Ash Wednesday)

- Gathering Hymn ("Ashes," Tom Conry, New Dawn)
- Signing in Faith/Sign of the Cross
- Opening Prayer (from sacramentary for Ash Wednesday)
- 1st Reading (Jl 2:12–18)
- Response (Any setting of Ps 51 is appropriate here.)
- 2nd Reading (2 Cor 5:20–6:2)
- Gospel Acclamation
- Gospel (Mt 6:1–6,16–18)
- "The Parable of the Two Stones" (See below.)
- Homily (Focus on the sign of ashes, the Lenten journey, and the ripple effect. Include an invitation to carry the stones/stone during Lent as a sign of the power God has given us to influence others by our lives and of our commitment to use that power responsibly.)
- Blessing of Ashes (pp. 76–77 in sacramentary)
- Ritual Action: Distribution of Ashes and Stones (After being signed with ashes, each member of the assembly receives two stones, one of

each color, to carry throughout Lent. You may prefer to distribute only one stone per person.)

- Prayer of the Faithful
- The Lord's Prayer
- Sign of Peace
- Closing Hymn (any appropriate Lenten hymn)

Note: The closing liturgy described below anticipated Easter for the high school students who celebrated it. We carefully weighed the issues involved and decided to do this for two very important reasons: (1) for a number of our students this would be their only Easter liturgy; (2) our service celebrated women's role in the Easter event with our all-girl student body in a way that would be lacking in many parishes. Your local community must weigh its own particular needs and circumstances in adapting the liturgy below.

The Parable of the Two Stones

(Dramatic presentation is an option; "Celestial Soda Pop" from a CD entitled *Deep Breakfast* provides good background music for either telling or dramatizing the story.)

Once there was a woman who had grown up under the care and guidance of her wise mother. When the time came for her to leave home she approached her mother with a request: "Give me a gift that will help me live my life as wisely as you have." Her mother had foreseen this moment and responded by pulling a small pouch from the pocket of her house dress. "Take these," she offered. "They have been the key to whatever wisdom I have discovered in this life."

Puzzled, her daughter accepted the pouch and pulled at the drawstring to empty its contents into her open hand. Two small stones rolled onto her palm and rested there, side by side. One of the stones was a deep, dark color; the other was bright like a light. Each of them was strangely attractive in its own way. "They're beautiful," the daughter whispered, "but what are they?" "Take them," her mother replied. "Life will teach you their meaning and purpose." "What if I lose them?" her daughter

7. The Ripple Effect: A Celebration of Connectedness

asked. Her mother reassured her, "These can never be lost. The more you use them, the more they will be yours."

The next day the daughter set out through the forest toward the village to begin her own life. After some time she entered a clearing in the woods and came upon a large, still pond of incredible beauty. She gazed at the pond, wondering how anything could remain so still. Even the breezes that swayed the surrounding trees had no effect on it. She searched the ground for something to cast into the water, but there was nothing around. On impulse, she thought of the gift her mother had given her. Overcome by curiosity she reached into the bag and removed one of the stones. She cast it into the middle of the pond and almost unconsciously took a step backward. Suddenly, beautiful symmetrical ripples began to move from its center where the stone had entered. The rings of water moved relentlessly to the shores of the pond. It was a beautiful effect, but somehow frightening at the same time. The pond seemed to grow colder and she felt a chill rising from the waves.

Afraid now, she hurried past the pond and out of the forest. Two days later she arrived at the village and began to look for employment. As she talked to different people she felt a heaviness in the air, as if someone had died. People seemed angry at one another and many spoke of hardship. She was about to give up and look for work elsewhere when a shopkeeper said a strange thing. "If you had been here two days earlier," she explained, "you would have easily found a job. Something's happened to this place and I haven't been able to put my finger on it. It seems like one thing led to another: a family lost their wheat crop, so the bank foreclosed on them, so they had to let their workers go, and then one worker got drunk and injured someone in a fight. It seemed to go on and on and touch everybody, kind of like a ripple effect."

The truth struck the daughter like lightning. She ran out of town and made her way back to the pond. The water was perfectly still once again, but it remained cold and threatening. She reached into her pouch, pulled out the stone of the opposite color, and cast it into the pool. All at once new waves were born at the center of the water and moved toward its shores. This time, however, the water became warm and inviting as the ripples moved over it. As the daughter watched she felt the warmth and peace move through her like a wave. Somehow she knew that things were already better in the village.

She had discovered the meaning of the two stones given to her by her mother. She only regretted that she had to give up the stones to find their worth. She sighed and lowered the open pouch. As she did so two smooth stones rolled out onto the ground, one dark, the other light. She remembered what her mother had told her: "These stones can never be lost. The more you use them, the more they will be yours." She smiled and bent down to retrieve the stones. She held them both tightly in her hand as she turned back toward the village and her new life.

Preparation for the Closing Ritual (Presuming Anticipation of Easter)

1. Prior to the day of this service, remind the community to bring the stones they have been carrying with them to the liturgy (have extras on hand for those who forget).

2. If necessary, set up the environment again as described above.

3. Place the Easter candle stand by the lectern and set the paschal candle itself where the entrance procession will begin.

4. Set the "mini-pools" ("terra pot" saucers) on the floor or on stands along the front of the environment for easy access by the assembly. Have enough small pools to facilitate a smooth procession and to avoid too many stones accumulating in any one pond.

5. Fill each mini-pond with enough water to maintain the ripple effect even after a number of stones have been dropped in.

6. If you can dim and brighten the lights during the service, it will add dramatic effect (see note below).

Outline for the Closing Ritual

- Procession (Lights are dimmed and the lighted paschal candle leads the procession. The bearer of the candle approaches the large pool and dips the candle into the water, creating the first ripple effect of

7. The Ripple Effect: A Celebration of Connectedness

Easter as Jesus did. The candle is then placed in its stand and the lights are brought up. Instrumental music or a hymn may accompany the procession.)

- Signing in Faith/Sign of the Cross
- Opening Prayer
- 1st Reading (Is 61:1–3,6,8–9)
- Response (Ps 104; setting: "Lord Send Out Your Spirit," Dean Olawski, OCP)
- Gospel Acclamation
- Gospel (Jn 20:1–18)
- Homily (The witness of the women at the tomb, especially Mary Magdalene, initiates the ripple effect of Easter.)
- Ritual Action: Furthering the Ripple Effect of Easter (The assembly processes forward; each person drops a stone into one of the small ponds. This action should be done slowly and reflectively, observing the water after dropping in the stone.)
- Processional Hymn ("Come to the Water," John Foley, New Dawn)
- Sign of Peace
- Closing Hymn (any appropriate hymn of your choice)

Note: The visibility of the rippling water to the assembly enhances the celebration. We discovered that if the lights in our worship space were reflected off the pools in the right way, the rippling waters "shimmered" on the walls and ceiling in a striking manner. It may be worthwhile for you to experiment with your lighting to see if you can achieve a similar effect.

8. The Cross and the Flower: A Lent-Easter Celebration

The following service works well for a large religious education or school family celebration because it involves family preparation at home prior to the celebration. Its symbols help families to ritualize their pain and struggles as well as their successes and joys. Be sure the family catechesis that precedes this service includes instructions about what to prepare and bring to the celebration. These instructions should encourage family dialogue about the meaning of suffering and resurrection in their own lives. We have done this service as part of a school Mass prior to Easter vacation or as a family celebration during the final religious education session before Easter.

Preparation for the Ritual

The main thing you need to provide for this service is a large wooden cross with a stand capable of holding it upright. The cross should be large enough to be a commanding presence in your worship space. The cross we made for this service was about seven feet high. Before the service it is necessary to insert small nails or tacks into the cross so that the symbols brought by the families can be hung from them. We have found that plastic push pins are the easiest to use, provided the wood of the cross is soft enough for them. You must have enough pegs on the cross for the number of families participating in the ritual. Once prepared, the cross should be placed in a central location in the worship space.

Each family participating in the service must bring two items:

- a small wooden cross, no larger than three inches (The family name should be written on the cross and a small loop of string or cord attached to the top for hanging purposes. The making of the cross should be a family project to allow for interaction and discussion.)

- an inexpensive fresh flower with at least three inches of stem

The ritual action for the service is quite simple and takes place during two processions. In the first procession each family brings forward the family cross and hangs it on one of the pegs. In the second procession each family brings forward the flower and places the stem through the loop on one of the crosses. The effect of the cross with the smaller crosses hanging from it and the cross with all the flowers added can be quite striking. Entire families may process forward with cross and flower, but it is also possible for each family to choose representatives for the two processions.

Outline for the Ritual

- Procession (It is effective to carry in the large cross as part of the procession.)
- Gathering Hymn ("Son of David," John Foley, New Dawn)
- Signing in Faith/Sign of the Cross
- Opening prayer
- 1st Reading (Ez 37:12–14)
- Response (Ps 23; setting: "Shepherd Me O God," Marty Haugen, GIA)
- Ritual Action: Procession of the Crosses (This action can be done in conjunction with or after response.)
- 2nd Reading (Rom 6:3–9)
- Gospel Acclamation
- Gospel (Jn 11:17–27)
- Homily
- Ritual Action: Procession of the Flowers (optional solo or choir piece: "Flowers Still Grow There," John Foley, New Dawn)
- General Intercessions
- Sign of Peace
- Blessing (A sprinkling rite may be used here, including a sprinkling of the cross.)
- Dismissal
- Closing Hymn (any suitable death-resurrection hymn)

9. Stone and Light: A Rite of Easter Witness

This celebration could be used in several possible situations. We celebrated it as the final prayer service in a high school before the students left for Easter break, making it our school community's celebration of the Easter mysteries. It could also be used in a parish setting as part of a Triduum observance. It is even conceivable that it could be incorporated into the Easter Vigil itself, with the newly baptized offering some of the witnesses which the service calls for. However it is used, the service should enhance or point to the Triduum rather than compromise or overshadow it.

This service uses two very basic Triduum symbols, the stone of the tomb and the light of an Easter candle, to ritualize both the personal and universal nature of the paschal mystery. Each of us carries our own weight in life; each of us has spent time in the tomb. Yet each of us has also been called forth from the tomb to lay down the stone and live in the light of Christ. This rite is specifically designed to involve each member of the assembly in simple actions that ritualize this journey from stone to light, from the tomb to Easter. The personal witnesses that are integral to this service affirm the truth that the Easter event is still happening in the lives of believers everywhere. The witnessing of these stories heightens the assembly's awareness of the Easter mystery in their lives.

Preparation for the Ritual

- a supply of palm-sized stones (2-3 inches in diameter), one for each member of the assembly (These are available at landscaping centers for low prices. Choose stones in a variety of colors and shapes. The size adds substance and power to the symbol.)

- a supply of white candles, one for each member of the assembly (Vigil light candles work best because they need to be left standing next to the stones after they are lit. We also found them to be safer and appropriately different from the tapers used at the Easter Vigil. Craft centers often sell these candles at discount prices.)

- something to place under each vigil candle to catch the wax (We bought inexpensive foil ashtrays in silver and gold colors. These are available at party supply stores.)

- containers from which to distribute the stones to each member of the assembly as he/she enters (We used plastic "terra pot" saucers available at nurseries or garden centers. Get enough containers to remain portable once the stones are placed in them.)

- a recording of "In the House of Stone and Light" by Martin Page from the CD of the same title (We included a dance prayer to this song to highlight the moments after the personal witnesses and ritual action. This worked very well in our high school setting but may not be appropriate in other contexts.)

- processional music either recorded or live (We suggest the soundtrack to *Henry V*, particularly the section of track 10, "St. Crispin's Day," which begins two minutes and thirty seconds into the track.)

- a variety of plants and large stones for enhancing the environment around the tomb (We rented plants from a nursery and bought stones from a landscaping center.)

- an Easter or "Christ" candle (Reverence for the symbols of the Easter Vigil will determine which candle is used for this service as the Christ candle. The integrity of the new Easter candle for the Vigil should be maintained.)

- a few taper candles to use for lighting the vigil lights

- people to give witness to their Easter experience (The number of witnesses will vary according to local pastoral needs and circumstances. As was noted previously, those who have been elected for baptism might be appropriate witnesses in some cases. Here is an excerpt from the invitation we presented to our planning group discerned as possible witnesses. Note that we chose a discernment process over the option of issuing a general invitation.)

The Gospel of John recounts how Mary Magdalene announced to the disciples the good news of her encounter with the risen Christ. The church has long since carried on the tradition of celebrating the resurrection through the personal witness of those who have experienced its power in their lives, such as the testimony frequently offered by those who celebrate the sacraments of initiation.

9. Stone and Light: A Rite of Easter Witness

Our Triduum services will include a number of individual testimonies to personal experiences of the Easter mystery, times when encounters with the Good Friday reality of suffering or death have given way to the light and life of Easter. We are looking for individuals who may be willing to explore with us the possibility of sharing such a personal witness before our community.

Here are some examples of the kinds of experiences that would be appropriate for these Easter witnesses: moving through the grief process after the death of a loved one; overcoming a time of injury, sickness, or suffering; growing from facing a personal challenge or struggle. In each case the idea is to emphasize the Easter experience, the new life or light that has been born of this encounter. Those who come forward will have support and guidance in the development of their witness.

1. If you are using a tomb, set it up first as a focal point of the environment. Place plants and stones around it. A worship space which can be darkened is ideal. Colored or spot lighting, if available, also enhances the environment.

2. Scatter a few of the palm-sized stones (the same ones the assembly will be given) around the entrance of the tomb. These will be used by the witnesses to initiate the ritual action.

3. Set up the lectern or an appropriate place from which the word will be proclaimed and the witnesses given. Make this prominent in your environment with the colors and flowers of the season.

4. Set up the Easter or "Christ" candle next to the lectern.

5. Set up the vigil light candles and their holders. Decide the location of the candles with two factors in mind:
    - accessibility of the candles to the people processing
    - how the candles will look in a particular arrangement once they are all lighted (We celebrated this service in an auditorium, so we set the candles along the border of the stage. Be sure to leave room in front of each candle for a stone.)

6. Place a few taper candles among the vigil lights for the assembly to use for lighting their candles (witnesses will have already lighted the vigil lights).

7. Divide stones equally in the "terra pot" containers for easy distribution to the assembly as they arrive. These can be left on stands to be picked up as people enter, but we suggest using ministers of hospitality to personally distribute the stones.

8. Give your witnesses final instructions. After the Gospel, a brief introduction to the witnesses is appropriate. Following this introduction the first witness comes forth from the tomb and moves to the lectern to speak. Afterward, the witness picks up one of the palm-sized stones from the ground around the tomb and places it in front of one of the vigil candles. The witness then lights the candle behind the stone, using a taper to take a light from the Christ candle. This action serves to model and initiate the ritual action of the assembly, which begins after all the witnesses have spoken.

To Build Your Own Tomb

Because we celebrated this service in a school where we were creating our environment from scratch, we built a tomb to serve as the focal point of our environment. If you are using this rite in a parish setting, your existing environment might render such a decision either redundant or unnecessary. Therefore, we list the materials for the tomb separately because they are optional. We have seen several types of tombs constructed as part of Holy Week environments in various worship communities. We present one possible blueprint here. You may have materials or ideas that are more suited to your resources or environment.

- seven panels of 4-foot by 8-foot "capri stone" paneling (Paneling is available at home improvement centers for about sixteen dollars a sheet.)

- several two-by-fours to serve as a support frame (Recruit volunteers with carpentry experience. Our tomb was constructed by theater department stage crew students.)

- enough opaque material to drape over the back of the tomb to conceal the opening

- tools for constructing the tomb (hammer, nails, saw)

9. Stone and Light: A Rite of Easter Witness

1. Build your frame according to the shape and dimensions you desire (we built our tomb in the shape of a trapezoid but we recommend a rectangle design for easier assembly), making sure to include enough braces in the structure to support the paneling all around.
2. One sheet of paneling forms the roof. Lay this sheet of paneling along the top of the structure with the four-foot width to the front and the eight-foot length to the sides.
3. Nail the roof panel in place on your frame.
4. Four sheets of paneling form the sides, two on each side. Lean two side panels against your frame at an angle so that together they adjoin the ceiling panel along its entire length. Nail the sides in place.
5. Repeat step 4 with the opposite side wall.
6. The final two sheets must be measured and cut into opposite right-angle triangles to form the front entrance of the tomb. Stand one sheet of paneling vertically against the left-front of the tomb so that the right edge of the panel forms the left doorjamb as you face it (you will have to determine the desired width of your entranceway). The outer edge of the panel should now be extended past the left side of the tomb because of the angled slope of the walls. Take a pencil and draw a line on the back of this outer edge using the slope of the side wall as a guide (this determines your cutting line). Cut the panel along the line you drew and nail it in place on the left-front of the tomb so that the angle of the cut edge matches the slope of the side wall.
7. Repeat step 6 for the right side of the front entrance to the tomb.
8. Take the paneling left over from steps 7 and 8. Measure and cut a piece of paneling to fit across the top of the door. This piece aligns with the doorjambs on the left and right and the roof at the top, and it forms the top of the door with its bottom edge. Nail this piece in place over the entranceway.
9. Drape two pieces of opaque material over the rear of the tomb to completely cover the opening. Allow the material to overlap in the middle so that the witnesses can enter the tomb from the rear without light seeping through. This preserves the illusion of an enclosed tomb.

Outline for the Ritual

- Procession (After all are gathered and everyone in the assembly has a stone, the lights are lowered and a solemn procession of the Christ candle through the assembly to its place by the lectern begins. Instrumental music or a hymn may be appropriate here.)

- Signing in Faith/Sign of the Cross

- Opening Prayer (optional original opening prayer below):
  > God of life,
  > You roll away the heavy stone of suffering and death
  > from our lives
  > and call us out of our tombs toward the light and hope
  > of resurrection.
  > Lift the weight of the hard and painful times of our lives
  > and light our path toward the goodness and freedom
  > that lie ahead.
  > We thank you for walking with us on our Lenten journey
  > and we praise you for once again bringing new life
  > out of death.
  > Like the women at the tomb on Easter morning,
  > make us faithful witnesses of the resurrection.

- 1st Reading (Ez 37:12–14)

- Response (Ps 27; setting: "The Lord Is My Saving Light," Andrew Witchger, GIA)

- 2nd Reading (Acts 4:32–35)

- Gospel Acclamation

- Gospel (Lk 24:1–12)

- Homily: Witnesses to the Resurrection (After a brief introduction, witnesses come forth from the tomb one at a time, give witness, and engage in the ritual action.)

- Ritual Action (The assembly is invited to process forward. Each participant carries his/her stone, places it in front of one of the candles, and lights the candle with one of the nearby tapers.)

- Dance Prayer ("The House of Stone and Light"; any suitable media, gesture, or prayer may be substituted here.)

- Sign of Peace
- Closing Hymn ("Awake O Sleeper," Marty Haugen, GIA)

10. Come Sail Away: A Celebration of Being Lost and Found

This Lenten observance continues to weave the symbol of light through the year's celebrations. Here we provide an opening and closing ritual for the Lenten season, again with the recommendation that you use opportunities to extend the symbolism into other aspects of your community's Lenten observance. One effective means of doing so is included in the material below. Because of the central and imposing symbol this observance incorporates into the closing rite, a symbol that strongly resembles the paschal candle, we believe that these services are more suited to academic rather than parish settings.

The focus of these Lenten rites can be summed up in the simple phrase, "Lost and Found," which probably planted itself in our consciousness because of the inordinate amount of time we spent looking for misplaced items as Lent approached. The foundation of this observance is the Gospel of "The Prodigal Son/The Forgiving Father," although we adapted it for our all-girls high school to "The Prodigal Daughter/The Forgiving Mother." The conclusion of this text provides the scriptural foundation for the phrase quoted above as the framework for this Lenten celebration: "We must celebrate, for this daughter of mine was dead and has come back to life; she was lost and is found." Fittingly, that concept is central enough to our faith and life experience to be echoed in other faith sources such as the hymn "Amazing Grace" and cultural phenomena such as "lost and found" departments in many institutions.

The Ash Wednesday service focuses on the experience of being lost and celebrates God's vigilant and active quest for our return. To place this concept in a context, we used sail banners signed with crosses to suggest the notion of Lent as a spiritual voyage, a time to check our compasses to see if we have "drifted out to sea," an invitation to seek conversion by turning our ships around and coming home to God's port. We found that this image of the voyage suggested the baptismal context of Lent while also providing a natural way to introduce the imagery of Easter light.

In the closing services, held prior to Easter break and Holy Week in our academic setting, the light of Christ is symbolized by a lighthouse, which rescues us from darkness and calls us home to safe harbor. We discovered that this combination of the "prodigal" Gospel story with the image of the voyage blended together well and effectively celebrated the Lenten journey and the Easter mysteries in a way that our students found fresh and engaging.

We hoped that it provided students who would not be celebrating the Triduum with a spiritual alternative to the cultural phenomenon of "spring break." For those who would be celebrating Holy Week in their parishes, we hoped that the baptismal rite and the paschal candle would take on a richer, more personal meaning.

Preparation for the Opening Ritual

- three six-foot lengths of one-inch diameter wooden dowel rods to form sail masts (All wood needed is available at lumber yards or home improvement centers.)

- three five-foot lengths of three-quarter- by three-quarter-inch plywood to form the cross beams from which the sails hang

- three five-foot lengths of one-half- by one-half-inch wood of your choice to form a weight along the bottom of each sail

- three banner stands in which to place the sails for display

- enough white material to make three sails, each one fifty-five inches wide by sixty inches long (The material should be heavy enough for the sails to "unfurl" when untied but light enough to "billow" a bit as they are carried through the assembly [we suggest cotton]. All fabric needed is available at sewing or fabric stores.)

- enough black satin, purple material, and gold trim to make three crosses in a pattern of your choice (We chose a Maltese cross pattern and made each cross fifteen by fifteen inches. Instructions for making crosses are found below.)

- three feet of Velcro stripping to affix the crosses to their sails

- about twelve feet of purple yarn to tie off the rolled-up sails along the crossbeam before they are unfurled

- an attractive book in which names can be recorded as prayer intentions (A *Book of Remembrance* is available from Liturgy Training Publications in Chicago. We made our own using a photo album cover filled with lined parchment paper.)

- a recording of "Come Sail Away" from the Styx CD *The Grand Illusion* or "L'enfant" from the Vangelis album *Opera Sauvage*

10. Come Sail Away: A Celebration of Being Lost and Found

- a recording of Paul Simon's song "American Tune" from the CD *There Goes Rhymin' Simon* (optional for dance prayer)

1. Prepare the masts for the sails by drilling a hole through the center of the midpoint of each three-quarter-inch crossbeam. Then drill a starter hole into the top center of each dowel rod. Lay one crossbeam across the top of each dowel rod and line up the holes. Now screw each crossbeam to its dowel rod using pointed screws and a washer. Tighten screws until all crossbeams are firmly attached. You now have three mast-and-crossbeam assemblies ready for their sails.

2. Cut the sail material to its designated size and sew a casing along the bottom into which you will slide the wooden weight.

3. Trace three cross patterns on the purple material in the style and size you desire (a Maltese cross works well). The pattern for the purple material depicts the actual size of a finished cross since it forms the border. Cut out the three patterns (we found a cardboard stencil helpful for uniform tracing).

4. Trace three identical cross patterns on the black satin, but make them one-half inch smaller to allow for a purple border all around. Cut out the black crosses.

5. If you wish, sew the gold trim all around each black cross. This is optional, but we found it very attractive.

6. Sew each smaller black cross (with or without trim) onto each larger purple cross, leaving a uniform border all around.

7. Sew small pieces of Velcro stripping to the back of each cross at all corners.

8. Measure each sail uniformly to determine where you want to attach the crosses. Lay the finished crosses on the sails in these designated spots and, using a fabric marker, lift the corners of each cross and mark the sail at the places where the Velcro stripping must go to match the Velcro on the crosses. Sew matching pieces of Velcro stripping to the marked places on each sail.

9. Place the wooden "masts" in their stands and hang the sails on them. A simple way of doing this is to drape about two inches of the top of the sail over the crossbeam and then attach it to itself along the

bottom of the crossbeam with four safety pins (this forms a casing of sorts along the top of the sail).

10. Slide a wooden weight into the casing along the bottom of each sail. Carefully roll up each sail, like rolling up a shade, and secure it by tying a length of purple yarn around it at both ends. Tie the yarn in a bow to allow easy release.

11. Set the stands in place where you want them displayed during the liturgy. Remove the sails and place them in back at the points where you want the procession to originate (we suggest using three separate aisles for starting points). Place the crosses near the stands, accessible for attaching to sails.

12. If celebrating this opening on Ash Wednesday, prepare the ashes and display them prominently in the worship space. The signing of sails in this rite intentionally suggests, and hopefully enhances, the ritual of signing the assembly with ashes.

14. Display the *Book of Remembering* on a stand near the ashes.

Outline for the Opening Ritual (for Ash Wednesday Celebration)

- Procession: Signing of Sail Banners/Blessing of Ashes (suggested music: "Come Sail Away" by Styx [for youth] or "L'Enfant" by Vangelis [for adults])

    1. Christ figure (presider or minister) processes up center aisle with rolled up sail, places sail in center stand, then unfurls sail by pulling loose the yarn.

    2. The Christ figure attaches a cross to the sail, then turns and beckons with arm gestures toward the other two sail bearers.

    3. The sail bearers process up their respective aisles and place their banners in the stands on either side of the center sail.

    4. The Christ figure assists the sail bearers in unfurling their sails and signing them with the remaining two crosses.

10. Come Sail Away: A Celebration of Being Lost and Found

5. The Christ figure or designated minister blesses the ashes by sprinkling them with holy water, then sprinkles the entire assembly.

- Gathering Hymn (any Lenten hymn of your choice)
- Signing in Faith/Sign of the Cross
- Opening Prayer:

    Loving God, today we begin the journey of lent, a voyage of rediscovery, of hope, and of new life.
    We sail onto the waters of baptism, the waters where our life in you began.
    As we set out in response to your call, we seal ourselves with the sign of our life in you.
    We also pray for the lost, the confused, the wandering, even as we recognize our own capacity to drift and lose our way.
    We pray that during this season the lost may be found and the dead may be brought back to life.
    May this celebration and this journey guide us home.
    We ask this through Christ, our Lord, Amen.

- 1st Reading (Jl 2:12–18)
- Response (Ps 23; setting: "Shepherd Me O God," Marty Haugen, GIA)
- 2nd Reading (2 Cor 5:20–6:2)
- Gospel (Lk 15:11–24 [The Prodigal])
- Homily
- Distribution of Ashes
- Hymn During Ashes ("Come to the Water," John Foley, New Dawn)
- Dance Prayer: "American Tune" (A dancer performs a free interpretation of this song which situates the melody of "O Sacred Head Surrounded" in a contemporary context. The needs and resources of the local community will determine the appropriateness of this music or dance.)
- Prayer for the Lost: Signing the Book of Remembering (Members of the assembly are invited forward to record the names of those they would like the community to remember in prayer during Lent. This book is then displayed in an accessible place throughout the season

so that further names can be signed in remembrance and prayer. Choir Music During Signing ("My Son Has Gone Away," Bob Dufford, New Dawn)

- Sign of Peace
- Blessing (A solemn blessing may be fitting [see sacramentary for Ash Wednesday].)
- Recessional (The sail banners lead the recessional forth.)
- Closing Hymn ("We Shall Draw Water," Paul Inwood, OCP)

Preparation for the Closing Ritual

- a lighthouse (Some landscaping centers or nurseries sell these, so it may be possible to purchase a pre-assembled one. Here is what you need to build your own:
    - four sheets of four-foot-by-eight-foot one-eighth-inch hardboard [about $5.00 a sheet at home improvement stores]
    - one sheet of four-foot-by-eight-foot plywood [price varies by finish quality]. We got medium grade for about $15 a sheet.
    - several lengths of three-quarter-by-three-quarter inch plywood
    - one three- or five-hundred-watt plug-in quartz floodlight. These are about $16 at many home improvement stores. We recommend the three-hundred watt model.
    - about six feet of clear plastic sheeting)
- a rock pool header (This is a water pool molded out of plastic to look like a natural rock formation. They are available at nurseries or landscaping centers and are priced according to size. The one we used held fifteen gallons and cost $35)
- a number of floating candles to place in the rock pool (You can find these at craft centers for less than a dollar each. Buy one for each representative participating in the ritual action.)
- music for "Candle on the Water" from the Disney film *Pete's Dragon* (This is optional for use with the floating candle ritual.)
- a recording of "Come Home to the Sea" by Chip Davis (This is found on the CD titled *Yellowstone* and several other Mannheim Steamroller recordings.)

10. Come Sail Away: A Celebration of Being Lost and Found

1. Purchase or build your lighthouse. Detailed instructions will not help unless you have people with carpentry skills. However, here is a general outline of our procedure:
   - We designed our lighthouse as a pentagon (a circular design or hexagon are also options). Our challenge was building one that narrowed as it approached the top.
   - We used the hardboard for the lighthouse's sides and the plywood sheet for its base and top. The top requires two pieces, one at the top of the walls for the light to rest on and one above the light as the roof of the lighthouse.
   - We used the plywood strips to make struts which ran from the lamp's base to the roof and formed a housing for the light.
   - The light rests inside this housing on the plywood base. You may have to build a smaller wooden base to raise the lamp higher off its plywood base.
   - The electric cord can hang down the back of the lighthouse or down inside it. We left the back of the lighthouse open (minus one side) to facilitate this. If you do this, of course, the back must be against a wall to remain invisible.
   - You may wish to tape some yellow plastic gel or cellophane to the front of the lamp to soften its light and add some color.
   - The clear plastic sheeting can be used to wrap around the lamp housing to simulate a glass enclosure.
   - Make sure your lighthouse is mobile and can be placed near an electric outlet.
   - We recommend that you use an extension cord that has an on/off switch which facilitates turning on the lamp.
2. We used a dramatic presentation for the Gospel of the storm at sea. If you have the resources for this, choose the players and schedule the practices ahead of time.
3. Set up the lighthouse in the worship space.
4. Place the "rock pool header" in front of the lighthouse and fill it with water. We added plants and large rocks around the pool for seashore landscaping.

5. Choose candle bearers to place the floating candles in the pool and give each one of them a candle. The number of candle bearers is up to you (we chose one representative from each classroom).

6. Set up the banner stands as they were for the opening liturgy and position the sail banners for an entrance procession.

7. Set up a stand for the *Book of Remembering* and place the book near the sails to be part of the opening procession.

8. Make sure Psalm 107 is included in the worship aid for community recitation in antiphonal style.

Outline for the Closing Ritual

- Procession (Unfurled sail banners lead the procession and are placed in their stands. The lectionary and *Book of Remembering* follow and are placed on their respective stands. Music during Procession: "L'enfant" by Vangelis or live instrumental.)

- Gathering Hymn ("The Lord Is My Light," John Foley, New Dawn)

- Signing in Faith/Sign of the Cross

- Opening Prayer

    God of life and light,
    We have made the Lenten journey on the waters of baptism.
    Now we gather in your presence to celebrate this holy week,
    To mark the climax of this passage from death to life,
    This voyage from darkness to light.
    Today we remember those who are lost in the midst
      of the storm;
    Even as we recall the stormy times of our own lives.
    Shine out in the gloom!
    Be a beacon for our deliverance!
    Bring us safely back into harbor
    To celebrate as one body the Easter mysteries,
    The triumph of life over death and light over darkness.
    We ask this through Christ, our lord.

- 1st Reading (2 Cor 1:3–11)

- Response Psalm (Ps 91; setting: "Be with Me Lord," Marty Haugen, GIA)

10. Come Sail Away: A Celebration of Being Lost and Found

- Gospel (Mk 4:35–41, The Storm at Sea; dramatic presentation optional)
- Homily
- Dance Prayer/Lighting of Lighthouse: "Come Home to the Sea" (Note: We developed a gestured dance to this Mannheim Steamroller piece to highlight the lighting of the lighthouse. The music is quite powerful and gradually builds to a high point which lends itself to the illumination of the beacon. The choreography reflected the journey from despair [being lost in the storm] to hope [revelation of the saving light of Christ through the symbol of the lighthouse]. After the dance the light can be left on through the conclusion of the liturgy, but guard against the light getting too hot.)
- Prayer of Remembering (Leader holds up *Book of Remembering* before saying prayer:)

    We pray for the lost;
    In this Easter light of Christ may they be found.
    We pray for the runaways;
    In this Easter light of Christ may they find their way home.
    We pray for the strangers;
    In this Easter light of Christ may they find welcome.
    We pray for the homeless;
    In this Easter light of Christ may they find shelter.
    We pray for the lonely;
    In this Easter light of Christ may they find love.
    We pray for the blind;
    In this Easter light of Christ may they find sight.
    We pray for the forgotten;
    In this Easter light of Christ may they find remembrance.
    We pray for the travelers;
    In this Easter light of Christ may they find safe harbor.
    We pray for all those in this *Book of Remembering;*
    In this Easter light of Christ may they find peace.

- Ritual Action (Group representatives bring forward floating candles; candles are lighted from the Easter candle and placed in the pond at the base of lighthouse. Song During Candle Rite: "Candle on the Water" [sung by choir]. If you do not use this song, which lyrically provides a context for the candle rite, you may wish to include a brief verbal introduction to this action [avoid undue explanation].)

- Prayer of the Assembly (Ps 107; alternate in antiphonal style.)

Ps 107: God Is a Refuge in the Storm (selected verses)

All: Let us give thanks for God's unfailing love,
for God's wonderful deeds on our behalf.
Let us offer thanksgiving sacrifices,
and sing with joy what God has done.

Left: Those making sail and going to sea
were voyagers on the waters.

Right: They saw what God can do,
what great wonders in the deep!

Left: God spoke and raised a storm,
lifting up towering waves.

Right: Their ships were lifted high in the air
and plunged down into the depths.

Left: In such danger they lost their courage.
They staggered and reeled; all their skill was useless.

Right: Then they cried to God in their trouble;
God rescued them from their distress;

Left: God reduced the storm to a whisper;
the waves grew quiet.

Right: They rejoiced at the stillness;
God brought them safely to the harbor they desired.

All: Let us thank God for this faithful love,
for these deeds on our behalf.
We must proclaim God's greatness
in the assembly of the people.

- Dismissal Rites (Sign of Peace, Blessing, etc.)
- Closing Hymn ("Awake O Sleeper," Marty Haugen, GIA)

Eucharistic Celebrations

11. Unless You Become a Child: An Adult Celebration of Childhood

This ritual was developed for use during a sacramental program for Eucharist as a way of inviting the parents of first communicants to rediscover the spirituality of childhood as Jesus invites them in the Gospel: "Unless you become like a child you shall not enter the kingdom of heaven." This ritual can be celebrated in two ways: (1) as a family celebration in which parents and children gather for prayer after separate sacramental sessions; (2) with parents alone while the children are engaged in their own prayer or catechesis. Which option you choose is a local pastoral decision. Sensitivity to separated and divorced parents is an important issue to consider. If the service is celebrated with parents and children together, it may be that both parents will be present, but only one of them will be seated with the child.

Preparation for the Ritual

- twelve vases

- one fresh flower for each family in the program (Two flowers are needed for divorced or separated parents. We recommend daisies for price and availability.)

- a tag or label for each flower to mark it with one of the twelve gifts of childhood which the service celebrates (Computer labels folded over on the stem work well, are easy to prepare, and the text files can be saved on a floppy disk for yearly use.)

- a table with an attractive tablecloth or covering

1. Print sets of twelve labels with one of the following gifts printed on one label in each set: (1) wonder; (2) joy; (3) trust; (4) laughter; (5) honesty; (6) curiosity; (7) spontaneity; (8) time; (9) simplicity; (10) openness; (11) imagination; (12) playfulness. The number of sets of labels you print is determined by the total number of parents who will receive them. Sixty families require five sets of labels; again, allow extras for divorced or separated parents.

2. Set the table in front of the gathering space, cover it with the tablecloth, and place the twelve vases across it.

3. Divide all the flowers evenly into twelve groups.

4. Attach matching labels to all the flowers in each group and place each group of flowers into a vase. You should now have twelve vases, each vase containing an equal number of flowers with identical labels.

5. Put water in each vase to keep the flowers fresh.

Outline for the Ritual

- Gathering Hymn (Incorporate music from the upcoming celebration of first communion.)
- Signing in Faith/Sign of the Cross
- Opening Prayer:

    Lord, we gather today to celebrate the gift of childhood as it is realized in the presence of our children who are preparing for first communion. May the beauty of their lives inspire us to recapture the grace of our childhood, to allow our children to be children, and to keep the gift of child-likeness alive in our hearts.

- Reading (Mt 18:1–5; "Unless you become a child")
- Brief reflection offered by DRE, catechist, deacon, or priest
- Celebration/Blessing of the Gifts of Childhood

    As each prayer is said, corresponding vase of flowers is held up.

    Wonder: We celebrate the childlike gift of wonder. May we keep alive a child's capacity to stand in awe of creation, to be dazzled by sunsets, to stare at anthills, to explore attics and basements, to stand in the rain, and to let our mouths drop and our eyes open wide in amazement.

    Joy: We celebrate the childlike gift of joy. May we share a child's ability to beam with happiness, to glow with excitement, to face a new day with enthusiasm, to cheer people up by our presence, to let sadness be overcome by a deep underlying joy.

    Trust: We celebrate the childlike gift of trust. May we learn a child's way of seeing the basic goodness in life and people, of taking a risk, of entering a relationship, of giving a promise, of

11. Unless You Become a Child: An Adult Celebration of Childhood

counting on people, and of firmly believing that most of the time God and other people will come through.

Laughter: We celebrate the childlike gift of laughter. May we know a child's power to laugh long and loud, to see the humor in embarrassing and difficult situations, to not take life and self so seriously that we cannot lighten up and laugh.

Honesty: We celebrate the childlike gift of truth. May we learn to be honest when it counts: to share our feelings, to admit our hurt, to offer our praise, to care about "playing fair," to follow the rules and standards we set up for others, to acknowledge our good and bad points and those of others without lessening our love.

Curiosity: We celebrate the childlike gift of curiosity. May we embrace the inquisitive nature of a child that asks "why?" or "why not?" just one more time, that questions how things work, that explores and takes things apart, that longs to learn about God's world and everything in it.

Spontaneity: We celebrate the childlike gift of spontaneity. May we reclaim the freedom to burst into song or laughter or applause, to jump to our feet, to dance, to give someone a kiss, to instinctively hug someone, to blurt out a compliment or a complaint, to cry without embarrassment.

Time: We celebrate the childlike gift of time. May we accept the gift of limitless time to do what really matters for others and for self, to take a moment to listen, to look at a school project, to shoot a few baskets, or to listen to a piano lesson. May we learn to be less busy, to know that there is always time to save for those we love.

Simplicity: We celebrate the childlike gift of simplicity. May we retain that ability to see things directly and purely, to shy aware from the complex and complicated, to be direct and honest and true, to not be a slave to figuring out all the angles, and to find God in the simple.

Openness: We celebrate the childlike gift of openness. May we see the value in testing options, in listening to new ideas, in trying new flavors of ice cream, in doing things differently than "the way we've always done it," in not letting sameness become boring, in opening our arms to embrace, our hands to support, our eyes to see, our ears to listen, and our hearts to love.

Imagination: We celebrate the childlike gift of imagination. May we never cease to enter that inner space where new worlds are born and new possibilities arise, where boxes become houses and crates become airplanes, where bold ideas are normal, and where limitations, obstacles, and ugliness give way to new power, hope, and beauty.

Playfulness: We celebrate the childlike gift of playfulness. May we catch our children's wisdom in not getting too caught up in work and business, in being able to waste time at play, in making time to recreate with family and friends, in not being too busy for others.

- Ritual Action: Distribution of the Flowers/Gifts (After all the prayers are concluded, catechists or children distribute the gifts, giving the flowers out randomly, one flower to the parents of each child. Parents are invited to develop, recapture, or keep alive the particular gift they receive as the day of first communion approaches. Music during action: "Unless You Become" by Alexander Peloquin, GIA [assembly/choir sings or recording is played].)

- Blessing and Dismissal

- Closing Hymn (music from the upcoming first communion liturgy)

12. Be the Light of Christ: A Family Rite for First Communion

This is a very simple service that you can use as part of a "kickoff" session for a first communion sacramental program. It provides an effective way to initiate the time of preparation for first communion even as it involves the parents with their children in that process. Our suggestion is that you use this service to conclude whatever program you have planned for the parents and children to begin their journey to first communion. This service celebrates the children as "lights of the world" for their family, parish, and world. Ideally, it helps to gently lead children beyond the idea of Eucharist as a private receiving of Jesus and suggests that Eucharist is a time to become more like Christ, a person for others. An added bonus of this liturgy is the fact that it unifies the process of preparation by bringing it full circle. The sign of the candle is entrusted to them through this opening rite, developed and reflected upon at home during the preparation time, and finally brought back to the church as part of the first communion liturgy.

Preparation for the Ritual

Assemble the materials and instructions for candle-making as given below. Place the candle kits in that area of the church or parish where the service will be celebrated. We placed them in large wicker baskets to make for an attractive setting and to facilitate their distribution.

- one four-ounce plastic glass to serve as the candle container (You can find these at kitchen supply stores. We found opaque plastic drinking glasses at a wholesale outlet store in red, blue, and gold that looked remarkably like vigil lights. Be aware that thin plastic cups sold for parties will not work because the wax will melt them.)

- one block of paraffin wax (This is often used for canning and sold in most grocery stores in one-pound boxes of five blocks each. The block should fit into the plastic glasses perfectly when melted.)

- one six-inch piece of heavy white cord or twine, the thickness of a candle wick (Real candle wick can be used if you choose.)

- one craft stick or popsicle stick (sold in bulk at craft stores)

- one piece of paper containing the instructions found below

- one Ziploc plastic bag in sandwich size to hold the kit

Instructions for Making the Candle

1. Attach one end of the wick to the bottom of the plastic cup with tape. The wick must be taped to the middle of the bottom so as to come up through the center of the candle in a straight line.

2. Lay the stick across the top of the cup and wind the other end of the wick around it so that the wick forms a solid straight line from the bottom to the top of the cup. Make sure excess wick does not hang down into the cup.

3. Melt the block of wax in a double boiler. **Do not melt directly over an open flame or in a microwave.** If you do not have a double boiler, place the wax in a tin can and lower the can into boiling water until it melts.

4. Carefully pour the wax into the cup. Put the candle in a cool place in the house so that it can set. As the wax dries the middle will sink a bit; this is normal. To minimize this sinking, save a little of the melted wax and pour it into the sunken space after the candle has set.

5. When the candle is completely firm, remove the stick and trim the wick to no less than half an inch above the wax.

6. Do not burn the candle. Make sure to bring it to the first communion Mass where all communicants' candles will be placed on a table and lighted.

7. If you have any problems making the candle, just call our "Toll-Free Hotline" (the religious education office).

8. If you want your candle back after Mass, label your name on the bottom of the cup.

12. Be the Light of Christ: A Family Rite for First Communion

Outline for the Ritual

- Hymn ("What You Hear in the Dark" [verse 1], Dan Schutte, New Dawn)
- Signing in Faith/Sign of the Cross
- Prayer:
    > Creator of all, we gather this evening in the light of your Son, Jesus, the light of the world.
    > As the day of first communion approaches we ask you to help us be the light of Christ so that we may brighten this world with your love.
    > We ask this through Jesus Christ, our Lord.
- Reading (Mt 5:14-16)
- Homily (brief reflection on the family journey to first communion)
- Ritual Action (The children process forward with their parent(s) to receive a candle kit. As the presider presents a kit to each child the following invocation is given: "You are the light of the world" or "Be the light of Christ." Note: In cases of separation or divorce there may be a desire for both parents to share the candle-making experience with the child. Giving out two kits, one for each parent, may be a solution, but it also weakens the symbol by creating two candles. Another approach would be for the child to work on a single candle with both parents. Obviously, sensitivity and communication are necessary to avoid undue hurt or conflict [e.g., a child with divorced parents receiving two kits could be embarrassing].)
- Closing Prayer
- Blessing
- Closing Hymn ("What You Hear in the Dark" [verse 3], Dan Schutte, New Dawn)

13. Gather Around God's Table: A Celebration of Community Re-membering

The rite described here can be used to begin any significant period of time shared by a faith community. We planned it to mark the gathering time for a school year, but it would serve equally well for an event like a parish mission, a workshop or convention, or even a liturgical season or year. The strength of the service described here is its ability to combine a festive atmosphere with a real solemnity. We celebrated it in a huge space that allowed us to assemble a community of more than two thousand students, staff, and faculty in one place. The power of the service and its symbols was certified by the fact that we were able to maintain the environment as sacred and engage the high school community in authentic prayer despite the fact that we celebrated in a gymnasium.

The foundation for this rite is certainly the eucharistic table of the Lord, although it is not intended to be a eucharistic celebration per se. The service finds its inspiration in the banquet feast parables and in the penchant of Jesus for making some of his most significant contacts with people in the context of a meal (Martha and Mary, Zacchaeus, The Lord's Supper, Emmaus).

This opening service focuses on three faith actions: (1) gathering the community to "set the table" for the new year; (2) celebrating the unique place of each segment of the community at the table; (3) setting a place at table for the poor. These simple themes are forcefully brought to life by the central ritual of this service, the very ordinary human action of setting the table. As our preparation and celebration of this service unfolded, we were aware of the rich and diverse meanings the symbol of the banquet table contained. Yet, we suggest avoiding the temptation to "bring out" the many nuances of meaning through undue explanations, multiplied prayers, or complex action. The table symbol is powerful enough on its own to engage the participants and allow them to process both its personal and communal significance. The following communique, which we used to invite and inform the community's preparation for the service, should clarify our approach (note that the students are one "department" represented by one of the twelve place settings, but segments of the community can be represented any way you wish):

Eucharistic Celebrations

Dear Students, Staff, and Faculty,

Welcome back. We hope that your summer was restful and enjoyable. Attached you will find an outline of the opening all-school service. The focus for this celebration, as well as for all our liturgies this year, is the symbol of the banquet table. The New Testament is filled with parables of the kingdom as a banquet and stories of Jesus gathering with the disciples at table. We begin the year in prayer with the symbolic action of gathering around God's table for the "feast" of the year ahead. This ritual celebrates our welcoming of one another, our nurturing of one another, and our commitment to include or "re-member" the poor at our table.

As usual, you are asked to help us prepare for this celebration. At the beginning of the service five tables will be arranged in the center of the gym floor. Each table will hold three place settings, fifteen settings in all, representing our twelve academic departments, students, staff, and administration. One space at each table will be left empty to be used as part of the intercessions. We ask each of you to take care of the following two tasks:

1. Obtain one complete place setting to represent your department at the table and one or more department representatives to put the table setting in place at the liturgy. Each setting should include a dinner plate, silverware, goblet-style or crystal glass, and a cup and saucer. These are the "minimum requirements"; you are free to embellish this basic setting at your discretion. A department member may already have an appropriate place setting to contribute for the liturgy (all place settings will be returned after the service). We will provide tablecloths as well as a placemat and napkin in a neutral color at each place. Please note that it is our intent to give the table setting a formal and elegant look to reflect the special nature of our first all-school gathering for the new year. While each place setting will be different, a reflection of the uniqueness of each department and the diversity of our community, we ask that it also reflect the formal and festive nature of our celebration.

2. Obtain a prayer of table blessing, a "grace before meals," and choose a department representative to offer this prayer at the service. Whether your department writes an original grace or uses an existing one, this prayer should be an expression of thanks and praise for your department's gifts and a calling forth of God's blessing upon the hopes and endeavors of your department for the year. A suitable prayer might be one which addresses two questions: What/who are we most grateful for as we begin the year? What/who are we most asking God's blessing upon as we begin the year? We will be happy to help anyone who needs assistance with this prayer. If you have any questions, feel free to ask one of us. As always, thanks for your cooperation. Your contribution adds a great deal to our prayer. We wish you a good beginning.

Preparation for the Ritual

- one table or several combined tables large enough to hold a place setting for each individual or group in your community (We recommend a round table if you can find or make one large enough, but combinations of other table shapes can also work.)

- a formal-style tablecloth for each table in your setup (We suggest a white or cream color depending upon the color scheme of your worship space. Suitable tablecloths can be purchased at department stores or made from material purchased at fabric stores. We used moire-satin material to make our tablecloths.)

- a cloth napkin and napkin ring for each place setting at your table

- taper candles for each table with candelabra or individual stands to hold them

- a centerpiece or accent for each table (At a craft center we purchased bunches of wax grapes in red, green, and black colors along with a supply of artificial wheat chaff for each table. We normally prefer natural materials, but we planned to use these items several times during the year and wanted to be cost conscious. We prefer the eucharistic association this centerpiece suggests, but other items could be effective as well. The wheat chaff served an important practical function in that we used it to dip in water and sprinkle the table as a blessing.)

- a small glass dish or bowl for each table to hold water for the sprinkling blessing
- a nice chair for each place at your table (No one will actually sit in these chairs, but they add to the beauty and genuineness of the environment.)
- one complete place setting for each place at your table (As a minimum each place setting should include a dinner plate, silverware, a cup and saucer, and a goblet-style glass. Anything beyond these minimum requirements is a matter of individual taste and discretion. While you may supply a uniform style of dishes for your celebration, we suggest allowing community representatives to bring their own place settings. The variety of table settings yielded by this approach more accurately reflects the diversity of community, and the elegant place settings people bring from their homes elicit personal and communal connections to the years of family tradition those dishes represent.
- one place setting for each group of persons being remembered in the general intercessions (The above minimum requirements apply here as well.)
- a small table for the extra place settings to be displayed until they are transferred to the main table

Two Weeks before the Ritual

1. Decide how your community is to be represented at the table. As an educational institution we decided that academic departments would be a natural way to represent the various segments of our community at the table. Students and staff were also represented by place settings. Again, depending upon the size of your community, other possible designations for representing your assembly are class levels, homerooms or classrooms, families, committees, ethnic groups, age groups, parish organizations, etc. As you can see, the possibilities are endless. If your community is small enough, each person can be represented individually.

2. Determine the size and shape of your banquet table based on the number of individuals or representatives at the service. Again, a round table is ideal, but a large number of representatives makes this very difficult. If you must use other table shapes, be sure to arrange them in a way that simulates a circle as closely as possible. The goal is to avoid having some places appear more important than others. There should be, for example, no "head" or "foot" at your table. We used five twelve-foot tables, so we found a pentagonal arrangement suitable.

3. Begin the process of obtaining dishes for each individual or group represented at the service. If you are inviting representatives to bring their own place settings, let them know ahead of time and give them guidelines regarding what to bring. (See sample letter above.)

4. Obtain or compose prayers of "grace before meals" to be offered by each group or individual celebrating the service. While sample prayers are provided in the outline, we suggest inviting representatives to offer an original or selected blessing which gives thanks for a particular gift and asks for a particular grace on behalf of themselves or their group. If you choose this option, representatives must be contacted beforehand so they have sufficient time to prepare. (See the sample letter which includes guidelines for choosing or writing such a prayer.)

5. Invite people to the service. Instead of the usual bulletin or school notice, a nice touch is to print the announcement in the form of a dinner or banquet invitation and send one to each individual or group celebrating the service.

The Day of the Service

1. Set up the table(s) at a focal point of the worship space.

2. Spread the tablecloth(s) over the table(s).*

3. Place the taper candles on the table(s) in the desired fashion. We placed four candles on each table, two at each end.*

4. Place any centerpieces or accents you have chosen on the table(s).*

5. Place a cloth napkin at each place at the table(s). An elegant touch is to fan or flare the napkins in a decorative manner.*

6. Place a small glass dish or bowl on each table near the centerpiece. Fill each bowl with enough water so that wheat chaffs may be dipped in it to sprinkle the table(s).

7. Set up the smaller table away from the main table(s), cover it with a tablecloth, and place the dishes on it which will represent those being remembered in the general intercessions.

8. Add candles, flowers, and other enhancements to the environment at your discretion. All other aspects of the liturgy should be clarified by the outline below.

*An option is to include items such as tablecloths, candles, napkins, and centerpieces in the procession and set them in place on the table(s) during the gathering hymn.

Outline for the Opening Ritual

- Procession (Instrumental music or hymn accompanies procession.)
- Gathering Hymn ("Gather Us In," Marty Haugen, GIA; include verse three.)
- Signing in Faith/Sign of the Cross
- Opening Prayer:

  > God of all goodness,
  > the eyes of every creature look to you
  > to give them food in due time.
  > When you give it to them, they gather it;
  > When you open your hand,
  > they are filled with good things.
  > Bless us and these your gifts,
  > which we are about to receive from your bounty.
  > Grant that as we sit down at table together
  > to share the blessings of this new year,
  > we may be shaped into its circle of unity and love.
  > We ask this through Christ, our Lord.

- 1st Reading (Prv 9:1–6; wisdom has prepared her table.)
- Response ("Taste and See," James Moore, GIA)
- 2nd Reading (Acts 2:42–47; they devoted themselves to the breaking of bread.)

13. Gather Around God's Table: A Celebration of Community Re-membering

- Gospel Acclamation
- Gospel (Lk 14:7–14; conduct of invited guests and hosts)
- Homily
- Ritual: Setting the Table/Saying Grace (Each segment of community sets its place at the table and offers grace.)

We set a place for science: We give thanks to the God of awe and wonder: God of the mystery and the miracle; engineer of the single-celled wonder and the intricate marvel of a human brain, the smallest speck of dust and the unfathomable reaches of a galaxy. We pray for the heart of a child: the ability to question, to explore, to discover. We believe that our search leads to a fuller discovery of God.

We set a place for theater: We give thanks to the God of drama: who chose to become one of us, who rejoiced to play our part. We praise God, who knows the pitfalls of life's stage and so nurtures our roles with wise and loving direction. We pray for wisdom to know our parts, courage to play them well, and integrity to be true to them. May our roles in life's drama teach us compassion for others.

We set a place for art: We give thanks to the God who is artist: painter of skies, sculptor of seas, weaver of fields, architect of mountains. Our God is the potter and we are the clay, the work of God's hands. We pray to the divine potter that we may be artists who see God's image in others and fashion all people into living works of art which give glory to their Creator.

We set a place for administration: We give thanks to the God of stewardship: who administers all things and directs the course of time and events toward ultimate good. We give thanks for God's call to stewardship by taking responsibility for the resources placed in our hands. May our leadership be marked with caring, vision, and strength as we multiply God's blessings one hundred-fold for the good of all.

We set a place for mathematics: We give thanks to the God of numbers: who adds to our days, takes away our sins, multiplies the loaves, and divides our sorrows. We rejoice in the power of numbers, sevens and twelves and threes, the numbers of God's life-giving action. We pray for the faith to know your most wonderful of equations: "Where two or three are gathered in my name, there I am with them."

We set a place for language: We give thanks to the God of language: the God who speaks to us in countless wonderful and diverse ways. We rejoice in the beauty of many tongues, many sounds, many voices. We ask for wisdom to understand that no tongue is foreign but rather an echo of God's own voice, a call to communication, inviting us to be of one heart and one mind in peace.

We set a place for English: We give thanks to the God of word and story: timeless truth, teller of tales, inspiration of the poet. We give thanks for the ears to hear, the lips to speak, and the hands to write the word. We seek the grace to be tellers of God's word and the compassion to live it faithfully. May the pages of our lives proclaim the truth with a full and free voice.

We set a place for theology: We give thanks to the God who is Mother and Father of all: present in every place, revealed in every face, giver of every grace. We give thanks for the presence of God's creative energy in this community, bidding us to recreate the world with the power of love and the peace of justice. We pray for the faithfulness to joyfully witness the humanity in God and the God in humanity.

We set a place for physical education: We give thanks to the God incarnate: the God who could not help but leap into human flesh and move among us with grace and power. We praise God in every straining of muscle, in each graceful arc of a dive, in the miraculous power of a leap, in the last-second surge for the tape. May our hearts be grateful in victory and strong in defeat and may we keep our eyes on the finish line as we run for the ultimate prize.

We set a place for guidance: We give thanks to the God of guidance: comfort for the weary, light for the searching, shepherd for the lost. We rejoice in God's gentle guiding hand in our lives. We pray that we too may shepherd one another,

13. Gather Around God's Table: A Celebration of Community Re-membering

freely sharing the wisdom we have gained on the journey. May each of us find our true and unique path to our one, common destination: the loving presence of God.

We set a place for business: We give thanks to the God of work: maker of worlds, parent of the carpenter, the source and end of all our efforts. We marvel at the ordering of the universe according to the divine plan. We pray for the Spirit who gives meaning to our endeavors, the ingenuity which animates our tasks, and the energy which readies our hands for the business of building your kingdom.

We set a place for music: We give thanks to the God of music: singer of songs in the bird and the whale, composer of music in the howling wind, keeper of time in the crashing tides. May we move in rhythm with the universe, live in harmony with one another, and follow your direction in playing your symphony of love for the world. We join our voices as one to sing your praises all our days.

We set a place for social science: We give thanks to the God of community: who created us as social beings, who dwelled among us, and who prayed that all may be one. We thank God, who gives us time and memory and culture. We ask that these gifts bring us wisdom to learn the lessons of experience, love to interact creatively with others, and justice to fashion a society that offers hope to God's people.

We set a place for students: We give thanks to the God of youth: a God ever young, ever vigorous, ever alive. We rejoice in the gifts of youth: its challenge, its energy, its idealism, its hunger for life. We pray for the grace to keep alive the youth within us, to be ever in touch with the power of dreams and the quest for a better world. May we be true to our dreams as we build that world.

We set a place for staff: We give thanks to the God who sees what is hidden, the God who looks beyond appearances and values the contribution of all. We give thanks for those who do the simple, the demanding, the taken-for-granted, and the behind-the-scenes tasks. We pray that such attitudes of cooperation and support may inspire all to greater generosity and unite us in the service of God's people.

- Final Table Preparations (Candles are lighted, table is sprinkled using wheat chaff. Hymn during preparations: "We Come to Your Feast," Michael Joncas, New Dawn)

- Blessing of the Assembly

- Intercessions: Prayers of Re-membering (As each intercession is read, a corresponding place is set at the main table for those being remembered, e.g., the poor, homeless, and hungry; the outcast, abandoned, and forgotten; our friends, families, and benefactors; former students, faculty, and staff members; those who have died.)

- Closing Prayer

- Sign of Peace

- Closing Hymn ("Table of Plenty," Dan Schutte, OCP)

Reconciliation Celebrations

14. Let the Valleys Be Raised: An Advent Rite of Reconciliation

This is an effective Advent service for young children from first to about fourth grade. It allows participants to act out the biblical call of Advent to "let the valleys be raised and the mountains made low." This service works best with groups of thirty or less. Its focus is reconciliation and the centrality of forgiveness to the incarnation event. We found that the visual experience of the effects of forgiveness which this service provides helps children to make the connection between reconciliation and the coming of Jesus at Christmas.

Preparation for the Ritual

- a long rectangular table
- a small stable with the figures of Mary and Joseph
- a supply of building blocks (If you don't have these available, "homemade" blocks are easily crafted by purchasing strips of two-by-two wood from a lumber yard and cutting them in two-inch lengths. You need one block for each participant and enough extra blocks to form a road from one end of the table to the other. We suggest about one hundred blocks for this liturgy.
- an Advent wreath

1. Place the table at a prominent point in the worship space with the longer side facing the assembly.

2. Cover the table with a tablecloth or attractive draping in Advent colors.

3. Set aside one block for each participant. With the rest of the blocks lay a "foundation" in the middle of the table and at each end. This foundation is only one block high with the blocks set closely together. Make sure there are spaces between the blocks in the middle and those at the ends (these spaces form your "valleys").

4. Place the figures of Mary and Joseph on the layer of blocks at one end of the table; place the empty stable on the blocks at the other end.

5. Take the blocks you set aside and stack them in the center of the table on top of the existing layer of blocks so they form a

"mountain" of blocks separating Mary and Joseph from the stable (be sure to build the stack in the shape of a mountain).

6. You now have the holy family on their journey to Bethlehem, but their path is blocked by a mountain in the middle and by the two valleys that flank the mountain.
7. Set up the Advent wreath near the table.

The Ritual

We will summarize the ritual here so that we can be more concise in the outline below. After a reading and reflection the ritual action begins. Each participant is called forth and invited to remove one block from the mountain (the mountain is made low) and place it on the table in one of the spaces between the blocks (the valleys are raised). With careful setup and some guidance during the service, the removal of the last block from the mountain should also form a completed road to Bethlehem, a path for Mary and Joseph to the birthplace of Christ. We found it helpful to do the setup in reverse, beginning with the completed road and moving backward to the mountain and valleys. This assured us that we had enough blocks and helped us guide the children in placing the blocks during the service if necessary.

Outline for the Ritual

- Gathering Hymn (any suitable Advent hymn for children)
- Lighting of the Advent Wreath
- Signing in Faith/Sign of the Cross
- Opening Prayer
- Reading (Is 40:1–5)
- Homily/Reflection
- Examination of Conscience (optional):

    Leader: We dig valleys of hurt with unkind words and actions...

    All: Let the valleys be raised.

    Leader: We build up mountains of anger that divide us...

    All: Let the mountains be made low.

14. Let the Valleys Be Raised: An Advent Rite of Reconciliation

Leader: We make valleys between us when we care about things more than people...

All: Let the valleys be raised.

Leader: We place ourselves on mountains of pride, high above others...

All: Let the mountains be made low.

Leader: We dig valleys of sadness when we put ourselves down...

All: Let the valleys be raised.

Leader: We build mountains that block the truth when we lie...

All: Let the mountains be made low.

Leader: We put valleys between ourselves and God when we are too busy to pray...

All: Let the valleys be raised.

- Individual Reconciliation (optional if time allows or if appropriate for age level)
- Ritual Action (Participants process forward, each removing one block from the mountain and using it to fill in the valleys and make a pathway for the coming of God.)
- Sign of Peace.
- Dismissal
- Closing Hymn ("Let the Valleys Be Raised," Bob Dufford, New Dawn)

15. Building Bridges: A Family Celebration of First Reconciliation

This celebration may be useful as part of an opening session for a family program of preparation for first reconciliation. It can also serve as a Lenten reconciliation service. This liturgy is designed for parents and children to celebrate together so that they may share the process of reconciliation. Each family in the community or sacramental program is commissioned through this service to build a small bridge of their own design and to bring it back with them to the reconciliation service (or to some other designated celebration of closure). Of course, "building bridges in our faith life" would become the focus of the entire program when this service is used. Its symbolic activity promotes the reconciling action of bridge building in the home, church, and community. When families gathered around their projects ask themselves, "How are we going to build this bridge?" an opening exists for them to ask themselves, "How are we going to build bridges in our relationships?"

Preparation for the Ritual

- several boxes of craft sticks (Enough to provide each family in the program with at least fifty craft sticks or popsicle sticks. These are readily available at craft stores.)

- plastic or paper bags to hold each set of craft sticks for easy distribution (We suggest plastic Ziploc bags.)

- two or three model bridges of your own design and making (This is important to give people both courage and inspiration for building their own bridges. We had fun making them in the office and were amazed at the many possible designs.)

- a simple set of instructions to be provided for each family (optional) (We didn't include instructions but displayed our model bridges and answered questions after the service. Remind families to use white or Elmer's glue and that thread or wire is an option for some bridge designs [suspension bridges].)

- a master "bridge builder's contract" to be photocopied so that each family receives a copy along with their building materials (A computer program like Broderbund's *Print Shop* is ideal for this purpose. Contracts might include a border, clip art of a bridge or other symbol of reconciliation, and a statement of commissioning in an attractive font [e.g., "The n. family is commissioned to build bridges for all God's people"].)

1. Divide the craft sticks into counts of fifty and place them in the bags along with any instructions or materials you have prepared.

2. Photocopy the contract for each family and fill in the individual or family name of each candidate for reconciliation or each participant in the service. Calligraphy enhances the contract; someone with that gift may be willing to help you.

3. Display all the building material packets on an attractive table at a prominent location in the gathering space.

4. Place your own model bridges on the same table or nearby in a highly visible place.

5. Prepare simple refreshments for after the service. This option gives people a chance to ask questions or share ideas. The room where refreshments are served might be enhanced with pictures or posters of bridges. Travel posters of San Francisco often feature the Golden Gate bridge. We found a marvelous shot of the Golden Gate shrouded in fog which gave it a spiritual quality.

Outline for the Ritual

- Gathering Hymn ("Hosea," Gregory Norbet, Benedictine Foundation)
- Signing in Faith/Sign of the Cross
- Opening Prayer:

    Loving God, we come into your presence this day to acknowledge what divides us. We gather to commit ourselves to building bridges to unite us with you and one another. Help us to overcome what separates us and to embrace Christ, who binds us together. Build us into living bridges that accomplish your work of reconciliation in the world. We ask this through Christ, our Lord. Amen.

- Reading (Jn 17:20–23)
- Homily/Brief Reflection

15. Building Bridges: A Family Celebration of First Reconciliation

- Blessing (Building materials to be distributed for bridges are sprinkled with holy water while a simple blessing is said over them: "Creator God, bless this wood and all who make use of it. May it be a sign of our desire to unite all that is divided, to reconcile ourselves with you and with one another.")
- Ritual Action (As names are called, each family comes forward to be commissioned with a bridge-building contract and materials needed to build a bridge.)
- Litany:

    Response: "We will build a bridge" or "We will be a bridge"

    Leader:
    - There are countries making war instead of peace... (*Response*)
    - There are families who are falling apart... (*Response*)
    - There are neighbors who do not get along... (*Response*)
    - There are friends who are fighting... (*Response*)
    - There are enemies who cannot forgive... (*Response*)
    - There are old and sick who feel abandoned... (*Response*)
    - There are those with no place to call home... (*Response*)
    - There are many things dividing God's people... (*Response*)

- Our Father (joining hands may be appropriate)
- Sign of Peace
- Closing Hymn ("City of God," Dan Schutte, New Dawn)

16. Lighting the Way to Forgiveness: A Community Reconciliation Ritual

This is a reconciliation ritual for a small community, whether a family, prayer group, base community, etc., that has experienced some dysfunction in the community because of an issue or problem that has caused hurt or dissension. This ritual is part of the rite of passage from that brokenness to the forgiveness and healing that can restore peace.

It is possible to celebrate this ritual in more than one way. Our outline begins with the examination and reconciliation action, then moves to the word: "Our actions have made the light of Christ in our midst 'go out,' so reconciling action on our part is needed to rekindle it." Yet, it also makes theological sense to engage in the readings and candle lighting prior to the examination and burning of papers: "The light of Christ has always burned in our midst and remembering its presence through stories of the word allows us to reconcile with one another."

Preparation for the Ritual

- four large candles and a taper candle
- matches
- slips of paper in two colors, one of each color for each participant (Avoid dark colors so writing is legible.)
- a pencil or pen for each member of the group
- a large dish or receptacle in which papers can be burned
- a warm, open environment in which to gather (This may include a table at which to gather [a round table is ideal] or comfortable furniture which is arranged to facilitate communication with a small table in the middle for the candles and receptacle.)
- time (This is not a service that can be rushed. The time needed will be determined by awareness of the issues and the people involved.)

Gather the group in the room or around the table. Place the receptacle for burning in the middle of the table or group, set the four candles around it, and place the taper candle nearby. The light in the room should be dimmed according to taste, remembering to leave enough light to read by. Of course, prior communication about the gathering will be needed so that participants

Reconciliation Celebrations

do not feel that the experience was sprung on them without warning. Provide each member of the group with two pieces of paper, one of each color, and a pen or pencil.

Outline for the Ritual

- Greeting/Introduction (Words may be needed to put the gathering in a context and to place people who may feel threatened at ease.)
- Centering Music or Prayer (Some vehicle to get the community in touch with its feelings and thoughts as the service begins.)
- Examination I (The leader/presider invites the members of the community to take the first slip of paper [color designated by the leader] and, after reflection, to write down a hurt or negative feeling they carry about the group or about life in the group as it is. This may involve naming individuals, depending upon the group's capacity to handle interpersonal confrontation.)
- Ritual Action I: Sharing of Feelings/Burning of papers (Members are invited to share something of what they wrote in some way; this can be done in pairs, small groups, or in the whole group. After sharing their hurt or feeling they are invited to use the matches and taper candle to burn what they have written. This proceeds until everyone who wishes to speak has done so. When the sharing ends, those who have chosen not to speak publicly are invited to burn their papers.)
- Examination II (The leader invites members of the community to take the other slip of paper [the other color] and, after reflection, to write down something they have done to contribute to the current breakdown of community or to the hurt that someone has experienced.)
- Ritual Action II (Penitential rite is said [e.g., "I confess..."] and each participant burns the second paper in the receptacle.
- Ritual Action III: Living in the Light (Group members proclaim the readings and light the candles. The taper can be used to light the candles. If possible, the first candle should be lit from the flames of the burning papers in the previous action. Subsequent candles can be lit from the first candle. Procedure:
    - Lighting of the First candle
    - 1st Reading (Mt 5:14–16)

16. Lighting the Way to Forgiveness: A Community Reconciliation Ritual

- Lighting of the Second Candle
- 2nd Reading (Acts 26:13–18)
- Lighting of the Third Candle
- 3rd Reading (Jn 1:1–5,9)
- Lighting of the Fourth Candle
- 4th Reading (Jn 8:12)
* Sign of Peace
* Dismissal Rites (Refreshments may serve as a fitting conclusion to the rite.)

17. Digging in the Dirt, Washing in the Water: A Rite of Cleansing

This is a ritual we have used with a high school senior theology class as a closing prayer service after a unit on sin, forgiveness, and reconciliation. It works well because it keeps the students involved in the ritual and because it incorporates music that they listen to outside of the context of liturgy. The service uses two songs from the Peter Gabriel CD entitled *Us*. The first song, "Digging in the Dirt," was written by Gabriel as he was coming to a sense of awareness and ownership of his abusiveness in a significant relationship. The second song, "Washing of the Water," is a song about healing. These two songs, used in the context of prayer, can support a real experience of reconciliation for adolescents. Be aware that some teens may not respond well to the slow, measured pace of "Washing of the Water." For these groups the more upbeat "River of Dreams" from the Billy Joel album of the same title might be the preferred option during the second part of the ritual.

Preparation for the Service

- a quiet, comfortable room where chairs can be placed in a circle
- Peter Gabriel's CD *Us* (Billy Joel's CD *River of Dreams* is optional.)
- a twenty-inch "terra pot" saucer or suitable substitute for holding soil (found in nurseries or garden centers)
- a large glass bowl or dish for holding water (Note that the size of the vessels for the soil and the water will depend upon the size of the group. We celebrated this service with groups of thirty seniors. The vessels should be large enough to hold ample soil and water for your group but small enough to be passed around the circle from one participant to the next.)
- potting soil or soil from the ground (Use enough to form a one- to two-inch depth inside the "terra pot" saucer.
- enough cool water to nearly fill the glass vessel (Too much water will cause spilling.)
- napkins or paper towels (optional)

1. Place the vessels for the soil and water in the center of the room. Place the soil in the "terra pot" saucer and the cool water in the glass bowl.
2. Make room for the participants to gather around the vessels in a circle, either on the floor or on chairs.
3. Place the CD/tape player where you can start and stop the music without distraction to the prayer.
4. Mark the readings and invite two group members to be lectors.

Outline for the Ritual

- Greeting (The procedure for the ritual actions will require some words of introduction. These can be issued as part of the opening comments or, as we suggest, immediately prior to the actions themselves. These words should be brief and not overly explanatory of the symbols.)
- Penitential Rite (Invite group to think of one individual they have hurt and one individual who has hurt them.)
- Opening Prayer (three options):

    1. "I confess..." from the eucharistic liturgy

    2. "A Prayer of Forgiveness" from John Shea's *Hour of the Unexpected* (Argus Communications)

    3. an original prayer of forgiveness and mercy
- 1st Reading (Rom 7:15–25)
- Response/Ritual Action I (The container of soil is passed around the circle. As the vessel comes around, each person pushes the fingers of one or both hands into the soil to the bottom of the dish. While their fingers are immersed in the soil they recall and repent an action they feel guilty about, ashamed of, or sorry for. Once they remove their fingers they pass the vessel to the next person in the circle. Be sure to instruct participants to hold their fingers in the dirt for several seconds and to be aware of their feelings as they do so. Also be sure that they don't wipe the dirt off their fingers once they pass the dish to the next person. The discomfort of the soil on the hands and the impatience to be rid of it are vital. Song during ritual action: "Digging in the Dirt," Peter Gabriel)

17. Digging in the Dirt, Washing in the Water: A Rite of Cleansing

- 2nd reading (Jn 3:1–7 or Jn 4:4–15)
- Response/Ritual Action II (The container of water is now passed around the circle. As the vessel comes around, each person immerses his/her "dirty" hand or hands in the water. While doing so they reflect upon God's mercy or recall a significant experience of forgiveness in their lives. Once they remove their hand(s) they pass the vessel to the next person in the circle. Again, instruct participants to keep their hand(s) immersed in the water for several seconds and to be aware of their feelings as they do so. Also, be sure they don't wipe their hands dry as soon as the vessel is passed. The feelings associated with the water on their hands (coolness, cleanliness, wetness) are vital. Since the water will gradually become dirty, it may be desirable to pass several vessels of water around the room. Another option is to have participants minister to one another by pouring water over the hands of the person next to them using a pitcher and bowl (we prefer immersion).
- Sign of Peace
- Dismissal

18. Opening God's Gifts: An Advent Reconciliation Ritual

This ritual is ideally suited for a parish reconciliation service during the Advent season. It uses a wealth of brief Scripture resources to inspire careful reflection upon God's gifts and deeper commitment to service for others by means of those gifts. It provides a healthy antithesis to the hectic pace and consumer orientation of the "Christmas season." It can also be easily adapted for local pastoral needs or circumstances.

Preparation for the Ritual

The only extraordinary materials you need for this service are small slips of wrapping paper and pencils for each member of your congregation and a medium-sized wicker basket large enough to hold all the sheets of wrapping paper you will distribute. The paper and pencils should be placed in the pews or on each seat prior to the service. The basket should be placed on a stand in the center of the worship space.

Outline for the Ritual

- Gathering Hymn ("Save Us O Lord," Bob Dufford, New Dawn)
- Introduction:

    During this hectic season our thoughts focus on gifts: gifts we buy and wrap, gifts we dream of receiving. Yet, it is so easy to take for granted the gifts we receive every day from God. In our prayers this evening, we reflect upon our failure to appreciate and use God's gifts.

- Liturgy of the Word:
    - 1st Reading (Nm 18:29)
    - Response (silent pause or psalm response)
    - 2nd Reading (Rom 12:6–8)
    - Response (silent pause or Gospel acclamation)
    - Gospel (Mt 2:9–11)
- Homily/Reflection
- Introduction to Examination of Conscience:

As children on Christmas day, we gathered around the tree, anxiously anticipating our gifts. As we gazed upon our presents, our minds wondered with delight: "What gift shall I open next?" We now recall the gifts we have received from God and consider how we have used them.

- 1st Reading (1 Cor 12:31)
- Examination:

  Lord, help us to open the gift of our hearts. The world today is so desperately in need of your love. So many times we do not care for the loved ones God has given us. Sometimes we cause them pain and anxiety. Sometimes we take them for granted or put our own needs ahead of theirs. We hurt those we should care for by our words and actions. Sometimes we are blinded by our greed and materialism. Our desire to own sometimes grows into an obsession. Our materialism blinds us to what is truly important. We focus on things and not people. We strive for possessions and not for growth.

- 2nd Reading (Rv 21:6–7)
- Examination:

  Lord, help us to open the gift of our eyes. Sometimes we don't look carefully; we don't see the wonder around us. We don't appreciate God's creation: we destroy our world with pollution; we damage our bodies with unhealthy habits; we destroy people by violence. We close our eyes to the injustice around us. We think we are helpless, so we do not even try.

- 3rd Reading (Mk 7:32–35)
- Examination:

  Lord, we thank you for the gift of our ears. Help us to open this gift to hear the cries of the hungry and homeless. They have no food or shelter, just a life full of fear. Do we listen to them? Do we hear Jesus? Do we remember the time when there was no shelter for his parents in Bethlehem? Do we remember a time when there was no shelter for us?

- 4th Reading (Chr 1:28–29)

18. Opening God's Gifts: An Advent Reconciliation Ritual

- Examination:

    Lord, help us to open the gift of our mouths. We are called to praise God for all that God has given us. So many times we are not diligent in our faith. We don't treasure the sacraments as we should. We forget that God is always with us. We turn to God only in times of desperation.

- 5th Reading (1 Cor 2:12)
- Examination:

    Lord, help us to open the gift of our minds. So often we shut ourselves off from new and different ideas. We distrust and reject other people because they are of different genders, cultures, races, or economic backgrounds. We see the differences but miss the similarities. We stereotype, we are bigoted, we are sexist. We cannot imagine how precious we all are in God's sight. We don't truly believe that every person is made in God's image.

- 6th Reading (Lk 6:36–38)
- Examination:

    Lord, help us to open the gift of our hands. It is only in reaching out to others in forgiveness that we can be forgiven. We prefer instead to carry a grudge, to build up walls. Sometimes we have been victims of violence or injustice and we refuse to forgive. We don't understand that our hatred and anger destroys ourselves along with others. At times we have not forgiven ourselves. We have not believed in God's forgiveness.

- Ritual Action (After a pause for reflection, participants are invited to take the paper and pencil provided and write down one gift they will give to God during this Advent-Christmas season or one gift from God which they will use more effectively in order to bring peace to their life, family, or world.

- Reconciliation (Each person is invited forward carrying the gift sheet they have written. In a few words each person expresses to the priest/minister his/her failure to appreciate or use God's gifts and the commitment he/she has made to do better. Upon returning to their seats after reconciliation, each person places his/her gift sheet in the basket on the stand.

- Prayer of Sorrow:

    Presider: Having recognized our sinfulness,
    we now kneel before the God
    whose generous mercy we seek.
    Our sorrow leads us to pray...

    All: Compassionate God,
    before you and before this community
    we fall on our knees in sorrow.
    Try though we may to live each day in your love,
    we cannot hide from our failures.
    Our sin is always before us,
    hurting our relationship with you and with others.
    Yet, all our hope is in your gift of mercy.
    And so, we firmly intend to reform our lives,
    to work for peace, to live in your love.
    This task is difficult, so we seek your constant help.
    Forgive us; wipe out our offenses.
    Cleanse us of our sins and bring us your peace.
    In your beloved one, Christ Jesus, is our hope and salvation:
    It is in Christ's name that we make our plea. Amen.

- The Lord's Prayer (or other appropriate prayer)
- Sign of Peace
- Blessing (The gift basket and the assembly are sprinkled or incensed.)
- Closing Hymn ("What Shall I Give?" Scott Soper, OCP)

Opening and Closing Celebrations

19. Knock and the Door Will Be Opened: A Rite of Beginning

This is not a liturgy so much as a way of using a central Gospel symbol in the service of liturgy. The ritual may stand on its own or be incorporated into a eucharistic celebration. If used in the context of a Mass, care should be taken not to make the door symbol into a "theme" because Eucharist has only one theme. Instead, the symbol of the door is a way of opening up the word for the community, especially at the beginning of a significant time or event (a new year, a liturgical season, or a common undertaking). Doors celebrate beginning, welcome, and a commitment to engagement on the part of the community for the time or task ahead. We first used these resources to celebrate the beginning of a school year. The rite emphasizes faith in the engagement process, the belief that the efforts of those who enter with wholeheartedness and perseverance are rewarded with fulfillment: "Knock and the door will be opened."

Preparation for the Ritual

- two or three decorative doors to set up as a display (We borrowed two beautiful doors with glass inlays from a company managed by the parent of a student. The doors are displayed prominently in the worship space as a symbolic focus for the Liturgy of the Word.)

- persons with drama skills if you choose the second Gospel (This text is well suited to the option of a dramatic presentation.)

- a recording of "Walk Through These Doors" by Marsi Silvestro for use in a dance or gestured prayer in conjunction with the presentation of the gifts (This song is especially appropriate for communities of women, but is rather difficult to find.)

- slides of various doors around your parish, school, or community (Our department chairperson took slides of significant doors around the campus.)

- recorded or live instrumental music as background for the slides

Outline for the Ritual (within a Eucharistic Celebration)

- Gathering Hymn ("Now As We Gather," Eugene Castillo, OCP)
- Opening Prayer (Use the Opening Prayer from Mass for beginning of the Civil Year #24 of the sacramentary. All prayers may be taken from this source if desired.)
- 1st Reading (Ex 12:21–23;26–27)
- Response (any setting of Ps 122)
- 2nd Reading (Rv 3:7–8;20–21)
- Gospel Acclamation
- Gospel (Mt 7:7–11 proclaimed or Lk 18:1–8 presented dramatically)
- Homily
- Intercessions
- Presentation of Gifts (Dancers may prepare the table in a gestured prayer or dance to the live or recorded music of "Walk Through These Doors.")
- Communion Hymn (any setting of "Where There Is Love/Ubi Caritas")
- Slide Reflection (Slides of significant doorways in the parish, school or community presented to the music of your choice.)
- Closing Hymn (any appropriate hymn of your choice)

19. Knock and the Door Will Be Opened: A Rite of Beginning

Options for Celebration

There are at least two options for celebrating this liturgy which you may consider depending upon the occasion, the size of the assembly, and the age group celebrating it. One option is to make or purchase attractive symbolic keys for designated members or for all members of the community. Avoid plastic or toy keys unless working with primary-age children. Keys appear repeatedly in Scripture, as in Matthew 16:19 in which Jesus entrusts Peter with the keys to the kingdom. This additional symbol may be well suited to a liturgy in which ministers are being commissioned, leaders are being installed, or new members are being welcomed. Be aware that large numbers of people make this idea expensive and time consuming. Also, remember that too many symbols in a liturgy tend to "muddy the sacramental waters."

Another option is to set up the doors in a manner that allows each participant to walk through one of them in the processional or recessional. In this way the community shares a ritual experience of the life experience they will share after the liturgy, namely, entering fully into the time or mission at hand. If you exercise this option, you may wish to place the doors in one location as a symbolic center and move them to another for the "entrance" procession. There is a potential richness in the prayer experience if the doors, having been present symbolically during the rite and "opened" through word and sacrament, were placed across the exits just prior to the dismissal. Every member of the community would then know the words of dismissal, "Go in peace to love and serve the Lord," as a true beginning, intimately connected to the life they now enter "outside" those doors. The cost and portability of the doors you use may influence this decision.

20. I Will Give You Rest: A Rite of Leavetaking or Closure

This brief ritual can be used with school, parish, or community staffs at the end of a year or just prior to summer vacation. It serves both as a rite of closure or leavetaking and as a prayer for a restful and re-creational summer. It could also serve well for any group that has just completed a significant endeavor or experience and would like to bring themselves to a sense of closure. The rite is purposely short because it was designed for use at the last faculty-staff meeting of the year where "brevity is next to Godliness." It may be augmented if local needs call for a longer service.

Preparation for the Ritual

- a suitable gathering space with a chair for each participant (Tables add convenience but may create a less open gathering space. The room must be large enough to set the chairs in several circles.)

- a collection of drinking glasses (Three glasses are needed for each circle of participants. Attractive goblets or drinking glasses are ideal.

- cold drinking water

- wine (A non-alcoholic beverage may be substituted, but wine is appropriate here for its parallel to the Eucharist.)

- a table large enough to hold all the glasses

- napkins (Have several on hand for each group.)

1. Group the chairs in circles of six to ten chairs each. The number of circles is determined by how many people you want in each one.

2. Place the large table in an accessible location in the room and set all the glasses out on the table in sets of three.

3. Fill the first cup in each set with cold water.

4. Fill the second cup in each set with wine or a wine substitute.

5. Leave the third cup in each set empty.

6. Place one or two napkins with each set of glasses.

Outline for the Ritual

- Gathering Hymn (optional)

- Opening Prayer ("A Psalm Before Leaving Work" or "A Benediction at the End of a Prayer Time" from Edward Hays' book *Prayers for a Planetary Pilgrim* [Forest of Peace Books] may be adapted for this purpose.)

- Reading (Jn 7:37–38 or Mt 11:28–30)

- Homily (A brief reflection upon the year or project just completed and the gift of re-creation that lies ahead may be appropriate here.)

- Gathering of Cups (Two or three representatives from each group are called forward to pick up one set of three glasses. Once they return to their groups, each glass should be held by a separate person.)

- Ritual Action: Sharing of the Cups (Depending on the group, something may need to be said about the gracefulness of "drinking in space," of taking a breath. Many meditations and exercise techniques specify the action of breathing well as a key element to their effectiveness. "Drinking" the third cup is simply a variation of that emphasis. Instrumental music may be played during the passing of each cup to enhance the experience.)

  1. Sharing the First Cup: A Prayer for Refreshment and Healing

     Leader: We pray for the life and refreshment
                   that water brings.
     We pray that the weariness and wounds
         of the past year will be healed.
     We pray for living water to well up within us.
     (Instruct the groups to pass the cup of water and drink.)

  2. Sharing the Second Cup: A Prayer for Festivity and Celebration

     Leader: We pray to be reunited with friends and family.
     We pray for the grace of celebration and festivity.
     We pray to remember the people, times, and places
         that make us human and holy.

20. I Will Give You Rest: A Rite of Leavetaking or Closure

           (Instruct the groups to pass the cup of wine and drink.)

    3. Sharing the Third Cup: A Prayer for Peace

        Leader: We pray for the time to reflect, and wonder, and savor.

                  We pray for the room to stretch out and the space to breath in.

                  We pray to be recreated, to be filled with the Spirit of peace.

                  (Instruct the groups to pass the empty cup and "drink.")

- Sign of Peace

- Closing Prayer ("Prayer to the God of Surprises" from John Shea's *Hour of the Unexpected* (Argus Communications) is an excellent choice.)

- Closing Hymn and/or gathering for refreshments

Note: Concern may arise about the healthiness of sharing from the same cup. We do not believe this service presents a health risk if celebrated responsibly, using napkins to wipe the glasses as they are passed. We also believe that drinking from a common cup is a stronger sacramental sign. Still, it is always an option to adapt this service if doing so will help allay fears and facilitate celebration.

21. The Tree of Life: A Celebration of the Circle of Life

This pair of rituals is well suited to celebrate a community's movement through an academic or parish year because the central symbol, the tree of life, signifies the rhythms and changes that are meaningful in our faith and typical in our life. As the symbol of the tree moves through the cycle of the seasons, it can evoke our natural human connection to the circle of life, the central Christian mystery of life, death, and resurrection. Furthermore, we found the tree symbol to have other benefits as well:

- It is a common and significant symbol in Scripture, with numerous references from Genesis to Revelation.

- The tree's symbolic impact can be sustained beyond individual services by making it visibly present to the community during the year.

- It contains natural connections to liturgical feasts and seasons that can be utilized for other celebrations such as "the Jesse tree" for Advent and "the tree of the cross" for Lent.

- The presence and power of the symbol can even extend beyond the particular year in which it is celebrated because it can be planted on the grounds of the school or parish as an ongoing, living reminder.

In one sense these services are straightforward and simple, but in another sense they demand a particular commitment because the use of a live tree carries with it some logistical challenges that require careful planning. The ideal is to buy the tree in late August or early September so that it can be used indoors for the opening service, placed outdoors in a temporary planter for the fall and winter seasons, and finally planted in the ground outside in early spring in the closing service. In this way the tree is alive with green leaves for the opening service, goes through changing and losing of its leaves in full view of the community, and becomes a powerful Easter symbol by being planted in the ground outside and watered just before it becomes active again.

Obviously, all of this takes time and research. We recommend working with a nursery to determine the size and type of tree that is best suited to your climate and facilities. There are several important factors to consider in your choice:

- Choose a tree large enough to be a striking liturgical symbol but small enough to get in and out of all the doors it will need to pass through, including the doors to your worship space, to the location of the temporary planter, and to the outdoor location where it will be planted in the ground.

- Select a tree hardy enough to survive the stress of being moved twice and spending the winter in a planter box.
- Consider your climate and its impact on your tree's life cycle; for those who live in a climate with little seasonal change this service may take on a much different shape or not work at all.
- Consider the liturgical calendar in relation to your tree's life cycle. The tree should be in the ground before it becomes active again, so a late Easter will make it difficult to focus your closing service around Holy Week.

The information and outlines which follow should address any other questions or problems you may anticipate. We begin by including the text of the memo we sent out to inform the community about the service and involve them in the preparations. Note that, for the sake of the ritual, the opening service situates the tree symbol in the Genesis context of a garden. Also, there is a reference in the memo to a tree banner. This banner is optional, but the resources we used for making it is included below.

Dear faculty, staff, and students,

On Friday, September 1, we will be celebrating our opening all-school service in the main gymnasium during a morning assembly. As usual, your participation in the service is appreciated and adds a great deal to our prayer experience. This year, the symbol which will provide the focus for all our liturgies is the tree of life. This symbol first appears in the second creation story in Genesis and reappears in the final chapter of Revelation.

The tree symbol will be presented at the opening service in three ways: First, it will appear on a banner that will lead the opening procession. This banner depicts a tree with leaves that gradually change color from the bottom to the top of the banner to represent the four seasons in the tree's life cycle. Second, long poles will be carried in and placed in a circle around the worship space. These poles will be wrapped with garlands of leaves for each of the four seasons (green leaves; flowering green leaves; red/orange autumn leaves; white, frost-covered leaves). There will be four poles for each season, sixteen in all. Finally, a large tree will be placed in the center of the gym as the symbolic focus of the ritual. This tree will be part of all of our liturgies during the year and will be planted on the property in connection with our Holy Week service.

In keeping with the Genesis creation story, our opening service will involve "planting a garden" in the middle of the gym floor. This garden will be composed of a variety of plants and flowers that will surround and enhance our "tree of life." The symbolic action during the service will be the placing of a plant of some kind in the garden by each segment of our community. So I ask administration, staff, students, and each department to choose a plant of some kind to place in the garden during the liturgy. In order to facilitate variety and uniqueness in the choosing process (so that we don't end up with twelve mums sitting in our garden) there is sign-up list circulating which allows people to see what others are bringing and choose accordingly (kind of like potluck). In making your choice we encourage you to consider three things: (1) variety (choose something unique and distinctive); (2) size (choose something large enough to be seen yet portable enough to be carried); (3) style (choose natural rather than artificial plants).

The plant you choose does not need to be carried in during the procession; however, it will be placed inside the garden during the service. We ask that you get two or three members of your department to participate in the service. One of them will carry in a banner pole with garland; the other(s) will place the plant you have chosen into the garden during the service. We will gather your representatives, assign them their roles, and arrange a brief rehearsal. If there are any questions, feel free to contact one of us. Thanks for all your help with the service and have a great opening.

Preparation for the Opening Ritual

- a tree (The nursery we contacted recommended a Norfolk sunset maple. Your ideal tree will vary according to your local area's climate and soil conditions.)
- four to sixteen wooden poles (We recommend dowel rods, ten feet long by one-inch in diameter, found at home centers or lumber

yards. Tailor the number of poles to your environment, but a multiple of four is necessary to correspond to the seasons.)

- a banner or flag stand for each pole (These can be rented if you don't have them.)
- artificial garlands in each of the following types: green leaves, flowering green leaves (ours had roses), autumn leaves, and white, frosted leaves (These are available at craft stores. We used eight garlands of each kind, two for each pole.)
- one plant for each community member or representative participating in the ritual action (Participants may obtain these or you can provide them. Extra plants may also be used to enhance the environment at your discretion.)
- a banner with a tree depicted on it (Your banner committee may be willing to provide this. We made an embroidery of a tree bearing the leaves of all four seasons in sequence from top to bottom. The pattern is found on page 147 of *The Pleasures of Crewel*, a publication of the Betty Crocker Home Library. The pattern found there is intended for a vestment, but we adapted it for our banner. This particular pattern is one option; you may have other resources or ideas. If you make a banner, you will also need an extra pole to carry it.)
- a candle with a tree image on it (This is another optional item which we used. Such a candle is available from the Acadian Candle Company in Richfield, Minn.)
- a large planter box in which to place the tree outdoors after the service (We made ours based on the dimensions of the root ball of the tree. The sides of the planter must rise a few inches above the root ball so that it is shielded from the elements.)
- several bags of tree mulch to place around the root ball of the tree after it is set in the planter (The mulch should completely cover the root ball in the planter.)
- a staple gun
- a recording of Vivaldi's *The Four Seasons* or the soundtrack to the Disney film *The Lion King* (*The Four Seasons* or the song "The

21. The Tree of Life: A Celebration of the Circle of Life

Circle of Life" can accompany the entrance procession or be used to choreograph a dance prayer for the service.)

1. Move the tree into a focal position in the worship space. Be sure to keep the root ball damp as long as it is exposed to the open air. We recommend draping the root ball or surrounding it with plants during the service to make the tree more attractive.

2. Mark out the "garden," the area where plants will be placed around the tree. Green or brown plastic or tarps can serve the dual purpose of protecting the floor and simulating the surface of the earth or garden.

3. Place the banner stands in a circle around the perimeter of the garden.

4. Attach one end of each seasonal garland to the top of one of the banner poles with a staple gun. Then wind each garland around its pole, stapling it in place as you move down the pole. Repeat the process if you are using more than one garland for each pole. Set the garland banners where the entrance procession will begin.

5. Determine the order of the procession and the placement of the seasonal garlands around the garden at your discretion. We chose to line up our sixteen banner poles according to the order of the seasons so that the sequence of "spring, summer, winter, autumn" was repeated four times. As our banner bearers circled the perimeter of the garden, however, they were instructed to place the poles of each season next to each other in the circle (the four spring banners together, etc.).

6. Attach your tree banner to one of the banner poles (optional). A crossbar may be needed to hang the banner from the pole. Set a stand for the banner near the ambo and place the banner where the procession will begin.

7. Designate an area near the worship space where participants can come ahead of time to drop off the plants they are presenting during the service. If you are using any extra plants which will not be part of the ritual action, position them in the garden at your discretion.

8. If you are using "The Circle of Life" from *The Lion King* for either a dance prayer or processional music, make the necessary arrangements.

9. Hold a rehearsal. This helps to facilitate a smooth procession and ritual action while providing an opportunity to drop off plants.

Outline for the Opening Ritual

- Procession (The tree banner and seasonal garlands enter to *The Four Seasons*, "The Circle of Life," or the gathering hymn. Processional music continues until all seasonal garlands are in place around the perimeter of the garden.)

- Gathering Hymn ("Canticle of the Sun," Marty Haugen, GIA)

- Opening Prayer (See the book *Earth Prayers*, edited by Elizabeth Roberts and Elias Amidon [Harper San Francisco], for suggestions.)

- 1st Reading (Gn 2:4–9; The Lord God planted a garden in Eden.)

- Response (any setting of Ps 66, 98, or 104)

- 2nd Reading (Rv 22:1–5; On either side of the river grew the tree of life.)

- Gospel (Mt 7:17–21; Every good tree bears good fruit.)

- Homily

- Ritual Action (Community members or representatives present plants for the garden. Representatives may be called forth by name and a brief prayer or blessing may be said as each plant is presented. After all plants have been presented, the tree, the garden, and the assembly are sprinkled. Hymn during sprinkling rite: "Rain Down," Jaime Cortez, OCP.)

- Dance Prayer ("The Circle of Life" or *The Four Seasons*)

- Intercessions

- Sign of Peace

- Closing Prayer

- Blessing

- Closing Hymn ("Sing Out Earth and Skies," Marty Haugen, GIA)

Introduction to the Closing Ritual

The closing ritual is actually more of a Holy Week ritual than a closing ritual for a year. The nursery we consulted informed us that in order to maximize our tree's chances for survival, it would have to be transferred from its planter box into the ground before it became active again in the spring. From a practical point of view, therefore, we could not afford the luxury of a May service. Theologically speaking, the early spring occurrence of Holy Week is the ideal time for the ecological nature of this service anyway. It made theological as well as practical sense for us to celebrate this service just prior to our Easter break.

In Chicago we have a summer festival called the "Taste of Chicago," in which local restaurants sell samples of their most prominent dishes in order to acquaint patrons with their menu and lure people back to their restaurants. The service which follows might be called a "Taste of the Triduum," a sampling of these most prominent liturgies of the church year. We are aware that a service like this runs the risk of exploiting, trivializing, or detracting from the importance of the Triduum. Using it raises the same issues that parish schools face when they decide whether to hold a Christmas pageant prior to Christmas vacation or a Holy Thursday Mass before Easter Break.

The decision to use this liturgy should be made with pastoral discernment of all the factors involved and with utmost respect for the liturgy of the church in general. We proceeded with the service that follows primarily on the basis of our awareness that many of our students had never celebrated the Triduum and would benefit from experiencing something of its ritual power. Just as the "Taste of Chicago" strives for return customers, so it was our hope that this "Taste of the Triduum" might draw our students back to experience the fullness of Holy Week liturgy.

Preparation for the Closing Ritual

- a supply of palms, one for each member of your assembly

- a table to represent the Lord's table and a suitable table cloth to cover it. (To avoid confusing the bread-breaking rite this service contains with the liturgy of the Mass, we do not recommend using the altar for your table. In fact, it might be best not to use the church as your worship space.)

- recorded music for the procession of palms (We played a recording of "Hosanna" from *Jesus Christ Superstar* to accompany the procession. Another option for a more adult assembly is "Hosanna" from Andrew Lloyd Webber's *Requiem*. Live music, antiphonal song, or a hymn are other options.

- loaves of unleavened bread, enough for each member of your assembly to partake (Several good recipes for unleavened bread are found in *Eucharistic Bread Baking* by Tony Begonja (Resource Publications, Inc.)

- an elegant serving platter for the main loaf of bread, enough wicker baskets to hold the broken unleavened bread for distribution, and a cloth napkin to line each basket
- a large wooden cross and a stand to hold it upright
- sheets of 8½-by-11-inch heavy stock paper and yarn or ribbon to tie them into scrolls (We suggest red paper or parchment and black yarn or ribbon. Each piece of paper should have the words "the crosses we bear" written in large letters across the top. This writing can be done in calligraphy or on a word processor with special fonts. The amount of paper and yarn will depend on the number of scrolls you need to make. See #11 below for details.)
- a supply of nails
- a cantor to intone and lead "O God, I'm Dying/Long Live God" from *Godspell* or a recording of *Godspell* if circumstances or preferences indicate this option
- several water vessels with lids, each capable of holding about a cup of water (There should be one container for each representative chosen to water the tree.)
- a fountain with running water (a still pool or font will suffice if necessary)
- several potted palm trees to surround the fountain or pond (These can be rented.)
- several Easter lilies to surround the fountain or pond
- a white cloth or sheet to serve as a shroud to drape over the cross
- an Easter or paschal candle
- an aspergillium or a tree branch and water vessel for sprinkling
- four podiums with microphones and reading lights
- ministers to distribute palms, proclaim the word, break and distribute the bread, carry the cross, nail the scrolls, facilitate or cantor music, sprinkle the people, and manage lighting (These roles are explained in the service outline below.)

21. The Tree of Life: A Celebration of the Circle of Life

1. Well in advance of the service be sure to: plant the tree, order your palms, bake your bread, build your cross and cross stand, and construct your fountain. Make use of the artists and craftspeople in your community to accomplish these tasks. The tree should be planted in an open area near the entrance to the worship space.

2. Prepare the palms for distribution at the place where the procession will begin. Assign ministers of hospitality to distribute them as the community gathers.

3. If sound amplification is needed in this location for the spoken texts to be heard, set up a portable microphone.

4. Prepare the appropriate texts in a binder and place it at the podium for the readers.

5. If you are using recorded music for the procession, make suitable arrangements for amplification. It may be piped over the public address system or played on a stereo system set up along the procession route. The music should continue in the main worship space until the entire community is gathered there.

6. Set up three podiums with microphones in the main worship space for the readers. Prepare the appropriate texts in three binders and place them on the podiums. We suggest typing and enlarging all the Scripture excerpts on a word processor and then highlighting the parts of each reader in his/her respective binder. It is also a good idea to attach reading lamps to each podium for reading in the darkness.

7. Set up the table, the cross stand, and the fountain at focal points in the worship space. These three elements should have visual balance in order to highlight their importance and relative unity. We suggest setting the table on the left, the cross in the center, and the fountain on the right so that the movement from one ritual focus to the next during the service can be smooth and natural.

8. Set up whatever lighting is available to you. We used an auditorium for our service, so we had the advantage of being able to highlight each symbol and ritual with theatrical lighting. We used soft white light for the table, red light for the cross, and yellow light for the fountain. If you do not have access to special lighting, find creative ways to highlight each ritual focus as the service proceeds.

Opening and Closing Celebrations

9. Cover the table with your tablecloth and place the wicker baskets for the bread off to the side of the table. Make sure each basket has a cloth napkin liner in it.

10. Bake the bread and prepare it for breaking and distribution. There should be one large, unbroken loaf on an appropriate serving platter (this is the "one loaf" referred to in the reading). Any bread that you will need beyond this main loaf should be broken ahead of time, placed in the wicker baskets, and covered to preserve freshness.

11. Prepare the scrolls that will be nailed to the cross. Prior to the service invite community members to write a personal cross on one of the pieces of paper you have titled: "the crosses we bear." They may write down a personal hardship, struggle, or loss (some may prefer to simply write their name). We prepared one scroll for each classroom and had each student write down one thing on his/her classroom's scroll. Other options may suit other circumstances. When everyone has written something, roll each paper into a scroll and tie it individually with yarn or ribbon.

12. Choose community representatives (one member of each class, for example) to present a scroll at the service. Be sure each representative is reminded to bring the scroll he/she had been given with them to the service.

13. Place the large cross somewhere out of sight in the rear of the worship space so that it is accessible when the time comes to carry it in.

14. Arrange palm trees and Easter lilies around the fountain at your discretion. If your fountain has running water, it is best to have the water running only during the Easter portion of the ritual. If your fountain has an electric pump it can be plugged into a power strip with a switch to allow for remote activation of the fountain.

15. Place the Easter candle near the fountain with matches nearby for lighting it.

16. Designate community representatives to water the planted tree. Give each representative one of the water containers and remind them to bring it with them to the service. Place the aspergillium near the fountain as well.

17. Gather all the ministers for the service and review their roles with them. We strongly suggest a rehearsal so that the ritual flows smoothly and prayerfully.

Outline for Holy Week Ritual

Part I: Palm Sunday (The Palm Tree)

- Gathering (Participants gather at starting point for the procession, and receive palm branches.)
- Call to Worship (Reader 1 reads excerpt from sacramentary for Palm Sunday.)
- Blessing of Palms (Reader 2 reads excerpt from sacramentary for Palm Sunday.)
- Reading (Jn 12:12–13; Reader 3 reads excerpt from Palm Sunday Gospel.)
- Procession to Dimly Lit Worship Space (Music, antiphon, or hymn accompanies procession. When procession arrives at worship space, all move to their places and are seated.)

Part II: Holy Thursday (The Giving Tree)

- Lights (Light comes up on the Lord's table. We suggest soft, white lighting.)
- 1st Reading (Jn 13:12–15; Reader 1 reads excerpt from Holy Thursday Gospel. Following this, minister at the table holds up the one loaf for all to see.)
- 2nd Reading (1 Cor 10:16–17; Reader 2 reads excerpt from Paul. Following this, minister(s) at the table breaks the bread. Ministers of hospitality distribute bread to the assembly. All stand and hold the piece of bread they have received.)
- 3rd Reading (1 Cor 11:23–24; Reader 3 reads excerpt from Paul. Following this, all partake of the bread and are seated. Light on the table fades; all lights are dimmed/turned off; the worship space is in darkness.)

Part III: Good Friday (The Tree of the Cross)

- 1st Reading (Jn 19:16–18; Reader 1 reads excerpt from the passion. Following this, a light comes up on the area where the cross will be laid. We suggest red lighting. The cross is carried in and laid in the lighted area of the worship space. Instrumentalist(s) and/or choir intones "Were You There?" during presentation [optional].)

- 2nd Reading (Mk 15:33–34; Reader 2 reads excerpt from the passion. Following this, representatives of assembly present scrolls bearing their personal crosses. Scrolls are nailed to the cross. Cantor intones "O God, I'm dying" from the musical *Godspell* [or other option]. The cross is raised; those who have raised the cross stand under it in reverence.)

- 3rd Reading (Jn 19:28–30; Reader 3 reads excerpt from passion narrative. Following this, all pause in silent prayer; all lights fade and the worship space is again in darkness.)

Part IV: Easter Sunday (The Tree of Life)

- Lights (A light comes up on the palm trees, lilies, and fountain. We suggest yellow lighting.)

- 1st Reading (Lk 24:1–3; Reader 1 reads excerpt from Easter Gospel. Following this, minister lights the Easter candle and drapes the shroud over the cross.)

- 2nd Reading (Jn 4:13–14; Reader 2 excerpt from Lenten Gospel. Following this, representatives from the assembly come forward and draw water from the fountain.)

- 3rd Reading (Lk 24:4–6,9; Reader 3 reads excerpt from Easter Gospel. Following this, cantor intones "Long live God" from the musical *Godspell*. All lights are turned on; the assembly joins in singing "Long live God." Assembly processes outside and gathers around the newly planted tree. Representatives come forth and water the tree with water drawn from the fountain. All participants are sprinkled with water from the fountain.

- Sign of Peace

- Dismissal

22. Building the House of God: A Celebration of Community Building

This is another pair of services that provides "bookend" rituals to begin and end a year or season in a community's faith life. We first used them as all-school celebrations to open and close an academic year at a high school. We found the "house of God" symbol to be a rich source of faith images and liturgical options. With these two rituals as touchstones, we were able to weave the "house of God" image into all our services for that year by using different rooms of the house as symbolic focuses for the seasons. For example, during Advent we celebrated the place of dreams—the bedroom—while Lent focused on the place where we welcome others, especially the poor and homeless—the living room.

This symbol can take you in so many directions; we recommend that you reflect upon the liturgical possibilities in the context of your community's faith life. We chose to use the architectural process of building a house as a symbol for the theological process of building community. More specifically, our rituals highlighted two main truths: (1) Every building reflects the values of the builders; we know what the community values by the things they "make rooms for" (make room for); (2) Every person or group in the community has value; each contributes a building block toward the completed house. When we communicated with school personnel regarding the rituals outlined below, here is how we described the approach:

> The liturgical focus for the coming academic year is "building the house of God." We celebrate the many ways that our life together and our cooperative efforts make a space in which God dwells and acts among us. The Gospel for the opening celebration is the parable of the two builders, one who built on sand and the other on rock. Through this ritual and throughout the year we will be asking the question: "What does it take to build the house of God?" In other words, "What elements go into constructing a place where people experience community and where God truly dwells?" When we met to develop this concept, two central ideas emerged: (1) The foundation for the house we are building is already in place; we need only to build upon it; (2) When we speak of building God's house, we are not talking about the

physical structure so much as the human elements that contribute to Gospel living.

In keeping with these insights, the service will begin with a simulation of a foundation already outlined on the floor of our worship space and fifteen rooms marked out inside the foundation. Each department is asked to choose a symbol that signifies their unique answer to the question: "What is essential for us to build the house of God?" or "What do we need to make room for (literally, 'make a room for') in order to build God's house?" The theology department, for example, could say: "To build God's house we must make room for prayer and reflection" and choose to display a Bible as their symbol.

After the homily, significant groups in our school community will be called up in reverse alphabetical order to carry out the ritual action. Fifteen empty rooms will already be marked out inside the foundation's perimeter. As each group is called forth, representatives will choose any one of the empty rooms and place a symbol within it that represents how that department realizes its value(s). When all departments have finished, there will be fifteen rooms or spaces outlined within the foundation, each containing a symbol of a "building block" that contributes to the completed building. A group member will say a prayer as that group's symbol is put in place.

It is worth mentioning two other options for the focus of this ritual:

1. This ritual is an effective multi-cultural celebration in a racially or ethnically diverse community: "In God's house there is room for everyone and we all cooperate to build our dwelling place." The symbols in this ritual could represent the rich ethnic or racial heritage of the peoples gathered to celebrate.

2. It could also serve as an effective ecumenical celebration: "There is but one church (one faith, one Lord, one baptism), where every denomination has a place and contributes to building God's house." The symbols in this rite could represent significant faith traditions or perspectives of the denominations represented.

General Preparation

To Build the Foundation

The symbol of the foundation which forms the heart of this ritual can be built to any scale you desire. The scale of the foundation should be proportional to the size of the worship space, the number of rooms marked out within it (i.e., the number of groups represented), and the types of symbols to be placed in the rooms. We celebrated in a gym with the entire school community, so our foundation was very large (27 feet by 24 feet). Fifteen groups were represented, so each room measured 8 feet by 5 feet. Be sure to sketch out your foundation and floorplan before you begin building the foundation. The perimeter is composed of individual three-dimensional brick props. These props are stood end to end in any desired formation to form the perimeter of the foundation. The more props you make the larger the perimeter of your foundation will be. We made twelve props to yield our 27-by-24-foot foundation. The extra three feet on the long side is due to space left for doorways.

- one 8-by-4-foot sheet of red brick paneling for each prop you intend to make (Brick paneling is found at home improvement centers for about fifteen dollars a sheet.)

- two two-by-fours for each prop you intend to make (eight-foot lengths)

- hammer and nails for attaching the panels to the two-by-fours

- a small can of brick red paint and a small can of black paint for painting the top two-by-four of each prop so that it resembles brick

- material for the floor (We suggest large sheets of heavy white paper from art supply stores or white poster board. Either can be taped together with white masking tape. Note: Making a floor is optional. You may choose to set your brick props on the existing floor of your worship space. Since the gym floor was not suitable for our environment, we chose to make our own. This was the most difficult part of our preparations, but the white floor we made was very striking.)

- something to mark off the rooms (We used bright red duct tape, but plywood struts, rope, or bricks are other options. The key is to clearly mark the rooms as separate when viewed from the assembly.)

Keep in mind that people have to move in and out of the rooms to place their symbols. Raised or three-dimensional markings will make this movement difficult.)

- symbols to place in each room (Having each group provide their own symbol facilitates ownership of and participation in the ritual. Encourage groups to choose creatively and to make their symbols prominent enough to be readily visible to the assembly. You might stimulate your community's choices by offering the following as suggestions:)
    - Theology: bread/wheat chaffs
    - Theater: an old trunk full of costumes
    - Students: a tree
    - Staff: various types of hats representing services rendered
    - Social Science: various timepieces (watch, clock, etc.)
    - Science: plants
    - Physical Education: a collage of an athlete's uniform, each part taken from the uniform of a different school sport
    - Music: musical instruments and a conductor's baton
    - Math: a calculator and an artistic representation of fractals
    - Language: a model of a bridge
    - Guidance: a box wrapped in giftwrap
    - English: books of poetry and literature
    - Business: a collection of keys
    - Art: an easel with canvas and paints
    - Administration: a statue or picture of the school or parish patron saint

1. Cut an 8-foot sheet of red brick paneling horizontally into four equal pieces, each two feet high. Some home improvement centers will do the cutting for a nominal fee.
2. Place one of the two-by-fours flat on the floor. Take two of the four cut panels and nail them along their bottoms to the narrow edge of one the two-by-fours with the brick side facing away from the board. When placed side by side the length of the two panel pieces should match the 8-foot length of the board.

3. Nail the other two cut panels along their bottoms to the opposite edge of the two-by-four, again with the brick side facing away from the board. Your wall should now stand on its own, although the top edges are not anchored.

4. Lay the brick prop on its side and place a second two-by-four between the loose panels so that it is flush with the top edges of the paneling. Nail the paneling to the board on both sides just as you did at the bottom. The prop should now stand on its own.

5. Paint the top of the upper two-by-four with red brick paint. The other board needs no paint because it won't show. Allow it to dry.

6. With the black paint, make narrow lines in the red paint, spacing them in brick lengths so that the top of the wall prop now looks like brick instead of lumber.

7. Repeat the above procedure for each wall prop that you need.

8. Stand all the wall props up and place them end to end in a square, rectangle, or other formation. We recommend doing this in advance because some props may lean a bit. Experiment with different arrangements until you achieve the look you desire. Our environment convinced many people that we had built real brick walls.

9. When you set up your walls, some of them will have hollow ends that will detract from the illusion of real brick. We suggest cutting lengths of two-by-fours, painting one side of each with red brick paint, and wedging them into any open ends of your wall props with the painted side facing out. You may need nails to hold them in place.

Preparation for the Opening Ritual

1. If you made a floor, place it in position in the worship space.

2. Mark off the rooms on the floor in whatever manner you choose.

3. Place the brick props around the perimeter at the edges of your flooring. Make sure to leave about three feet on each of two opposite sides for doorways. Cover the open ends of the brick props with the wood blocks you have prepared.

4. Have group representatives bring their symbols to the worship space beforehand so that they can be attractively placed around the outside of the foundation. We put name cards on the floor to indicate for each group where to leave the symbols.

5. Inform each group to choose two or three representatives for the ritual action: one or two to place the symbol in the room and one to

read the prayer at the podium while the symbol is placed. It does not matter which symbol goes in which room; however, we chose to put the theology symbol in the center of the building.

6. Decide upon a procedure for blessing the rooms at the end of the ritual. One option is to have the presider sprinkle or incense all the rooms. Another option is to have a leader from each group come forward for the blessing and pass the incense or holy water among them as each blesses his/her respective room.

7. Place your aspergillium or censer (whichever you are using for the blessing of rooms) in an accessible place.

Outline for the Opening Ritual

- Optional Procession (House symbols may be carried in and placed around the perimeter of the foundation, or the symbols may be set in place prior to the liturgy.)

- Gathering Hymn ("In This House," Marylu Hill, Evensong, or "God is Building a House," Carey Landry, New Dawn)

- Signing in Faith/Sign of the Cross

- Opening Prayer (Use the following or adapt prayers from "Common for the Dedication of a Church" in the sacramentary:)

    Creator of all,
    we come before you today
    with plans for the year and dreams for our future.
    Fashion these hopes into a blueprint for our lives
    so that we may build our house on the foundation of your love,
    in the vision of Jesus,
    and with the energy of the Spirit.
    As you have made room for us in your dwelling,
    so may we make room for you in our hearts
    by welcoming those who seek shelter.
    Build us up into a dwelling place for the Spirit
    where all may find their home in you.

- 1st Reading (1 Kgs 8:22–29)

- Response (Ps 27; setting: "If the Lord Does Not Build," Dan Schutte, New Dawn)

- 2nd Reading (Eph 2:19–22)
- Gospel Acclamation
- Gospel (Mt 7:24–27)
- Homily
- Ritual Action (Each group being represented is called forth by name. Symbols are placed in each room by group representatives. A prayer for each group is said as their symbol is placed in the house:)

    Theology: We make room in our house for nourishment of body and spirit. May our minds and hearts be filled with the grace of God and the wisdom of our ancestors. May the bread we break enrich our poverty of spirit and strengthen our poverty of body, forming us more completely into the one body of Christ.

    Theater: We make room in our house for storytelling, for sharing our human emotions and histories. May these stories passed down through the ages make us more human and lead us to compassion for others and celebration of the richness of the human drama where God is ever present and active.

    Students: We make room in our house for growth, hopes, and dreams. This year may we grow in unity, reaching out to accept and help each other; may we live each day with the hope in our hearts to transform the world with a Christian spirit; may we accomplish many goals, working hard and struggling to make our dreams come true.

    Staff: We make room in our house for hospitality. May our house be always prepared to welcome others. May we make one another at home and open our doors to those who seek the comfort of a well-prepared house and the service that embodies God's ever-welcoming spirit.

    Social Science: We make room in our house for time. May our preservation of and reflection on the memories of the past provide a gateway to a brighter future so that all may grow in wisdom and teach future generations the joys and sorrows of living a fully human life.

Science: We make room in our house for nurturing the life process. May we always stand in awe of the miracles of creation and respond with increasing reverence for all forms of life. May the marvels of the universe lead us to care for the earth upon which our house rests, feeding her as she feeds us.

Physical Education: We make room in our house for recreation. May our bodies become graceful channels of God's spirit, playing with the abandonment of pure freedom and striving with the force of utter commitment. May our spirits be recreated as we face life's triumphs humbly and life's defeats courageously.

Music: We make room in our house for harmony. May our hearts learn to sing their own songs, remaining in rhythm with the beat of the universe and in tune with the music of others. May the God who hears the beauty in every note direct us all in a symphony of the universe, a song of the soul.

Math: We make room in our house for order. As mathematics brings order out of the chaos of fractals, so may we respond to the chaotic and unpredictable nature of our existence with a vision of the beauty of life and the discipline that strives to bring clarity and meaning out of confusion.

Language: We make room in our house for communication. May we reach out across barriers of culture and language to bridge the gaps that separate people so that we may be aware of the boundless ways in which God speaks to us through the rich diversity of human words and customs.

Guidance: We make room in our house for discovery. May we appreciate the many gifts in ourselves and others. Let us come to understand who we are now and who we are becoming, thankful for the light of God which is reflected in each of us.

English: We make room in our house for poetry. May the rhyme of words and the reason of language lead us ever more deeply to understand ourselves and to identify with the struggles of others. May God's gift of language and lyricism give meaning and direction to the human adventure.

Business: We make room in our house for the future. May the skills we develop in the present be the key which opens doorways to a bright and promising future. May we use our talents and gifts responsibly and so lend stability and strength to a world that is ever new and ever changing.

Art: We make room in our house for beauty. May we appreciate the care and graciousness of God the artist, who takes us beyond the pragmatic and the restrained and leads us into realms of extravagance and boldness, recognizing the power of color and form to open our eyes to new possibilities.

Administration: We make room in our house for dreams. May the charism of leadership empower the dreamer in us all and break through the limits of time and space to create new hopes and achievements. May God the dreamer transform our future in the goals and dreams we weave in this present moment.

- Petitions (Response: Build us up into the house of God.)
- Blessing Rite (Each room of the house is blessed; the assembly is blessed [choose sprinkling or incense rite].)
- Hymn during Blessing ("I Rejoiced," John Foley, New Dawn)
- Closing Hymn ("City Of God," Dan Schutte, New Dawn)

Preparation for the Closing Ritual

Preparation for the closing rite is exactly like the preparation for the opening rite except that the flow of the action is reversed. In this ritual the symbols will be taken out of the house rather than carried into it: "We go forth to build God's house beyond these walls." Therefore, group representatives are instructed to place their symbols inside the rooms for the beginning of the ritual and carry them out as part of the closing procession. Because of circumstances, we celebrated this closing service in the context of an Ascension Thursday Mass. While this is not ideal, the theological and liturgical focus of the Ascension was very much in tune with the focus of this service.

Be sure to inform group leaders to obtain two representatives who will gather in the rooms next to their symbols just before the final blessing. When the closing hymn begins the representatives pick up their symbols and carry them out of the worship space. You will also need enough volunteers to carry the entire foundation out during the recessional. Two volunteers are assigned to each brick prop, one to carry each end. If you have made a removable floor, we recommend that you have people on hand to roll it up and carry it out as well. We congratulated ourselves that we finally managed to plan a celebration that includes cleanup as part of the ritual!

Outline for the Closing Ritual (Celebrated on Ascension Thursday)

- Greeting/Introduction

    Good morning! As the year we have shared comes to a close, we gather to celebrate the feast of the Ascension of our Lord. We have joined our efforts throughout this year to build the house of God. Today Christ bids us to go forth beyond the walls of this place and continue to build God's house, to shelter God's people, and to bring forth God's kingdom.

- Gathering Hymn ("To You O God I Lift Up My Soul," Bob Hurd, OCP)

- Signing in Faith/Sign of the Cross

- Opening Prayer (Prayer of the day in sacramentary)

- 1st Reading (Acts 1:1–11)

- Response (Ps 122; setting: "I Rejoiced," John Foley, New Dawn)

- 2nd Reading (Eph 1:17–23)

- Gospel Acclamation

- Gospel (Mt 28:16–20)

- Homily

    We take leave of one another. We accept the call to be "the body of Christ" on earth. We take down the house and go forth to build the kingdom

- Prayer of the Faithful

- Presentation of Gifts ("Be Not Afraid," Bob Dufford, New Dawn)

- Communion Hymn ("Blest Are They," David Haas, GIA)

- Dismissal Rite/Commissioning

    As we sing our closing hymn, we carry forth the house we have built, the symbols of the dreams and goals our common efforts have realized. Now God's house lives in us! We carry it forth to be a foundation of shelter and hope for the whole world. We invite all God's people to join us in continuing to build God's kingdom.

- Recessional ("Bring Forth the Kingdom," Marty Haugen, GIA)

- Ritual Action (As the closing hymn is sung, members of each group remove their respective symbols from their rooms and carry them out of the worship space, symbolic of the community's willingness to take the dreams and goals they have built up during the year and build them in the larger community and the world.)

Miscellaneous Celebrations

23. Sharing the Seed of God's Blessings: A Celebration of Thanksgiving

This ritual symbolizes the dynamics of Christian giving in an experiential manner, appealing especially to the senses of sight and sound. It may be used as part of a Thanksgiving service in a school or religious education setting where the community celebrates a liturgy prior to dismissal for the holiday. It can also serve as a prayer of thanks at other times, especially when there is a desire to call the community to share its blessings.

The ritual in this service engages the participants in a simple act of sharing (pouring a small portion of grain into a bin) and immediately fulfills that action with tangible results (the overflowing of that gift into the lives of others). In that sense, the ritual is a microcosm of the dynamic of thanksgiving, an accelerated version of a process that begins with personal generosity and culminates in a sign of the kingdom. The service also includes an offering of canned goods for a food pantry so that the playful aspect of the service is balanced by concrete action on behalf of the poor. We have found that this ritual works best with children of grammar-school age, especially as a family celebration.

The ritual described here depends upon the construction of a "Rube Goldberg" type of device that has its origin in memories of child's play. As children we used to take several half-gallon milk cartons and place them on graduated levels of our front porch steps. We would cut off the tops of all the cartons and punch a small round hole on one side of each one. Next we would insert one end of a drinking straw into each hole and extend the other end over the top of the carton on the next lowest level. The straw from the lowest carton would extend over a bucket which rested on the bottom step. When everything was ready we would turn on the hose, begin pouring water into the uppermost carton, and the fun would begin. (I guess we were easily amused.) As each carton filled up the water would overflow into the next carton through the drinking straw. This would proceed until a continuous flow was established with each carton flowing into the next and the water coming to rest in the bucket. We hope this provides you with a mental picture of how the device described below is intended to operate (see diagram).

Miscellaneous Celebrations

Preparation for the Ritual

- two large bins capable of holding all the grain

- four small cartons or containers for the grain to move through (We suggest half-gallon milk or juice cartons. Have extra cartons on hand in case of mistakes.)

- four plastic or cardboard tubes capable of conducting the flow of grain from one carton to the next (Do not cut the tubes until you know how long they need to be.)

- four stands of graduated height upon which to rest the cartons so they decrease in height from left to right (see diagram)

- decorative contact paper or other covering for the cartons

- a roll of masking tape or duct tape

- artwork or symbols to place on the front of the cartons to suggest what each represents (Our four cartons represented home,

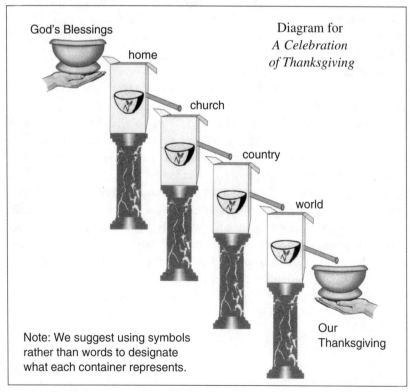

Diagram for *A Celebration of Thanksgiving*

God's Blessings
home
church
country
world
Our Thanksgiving

Note: We suggest using symbols rather than words to designate what each container represents.

23. Sharing the Seed of God's Blessings: A Celebration of Thanksgiving

church/parish, nation, and world. You may use these or choose other scenarios.)

- artwork or symbols to place on the two large bins to suggest what each represents (We recommend an outstretched hand bearing grain for one bin and an outstretched empty hand for the other.)
- attractive drapings to place over the stands (We covered our stands to disguise their makeshift nature.)
- a supply of grain seed sufficient for the size of your assembly (There should be enough for each participant to place a small cup of grain into the first bin.)
- one or more three- to four-ounce cups for scooping the grain into the bin

1. Determine a central location in the worship space for the setup.

2. Set the first large bin on the floor at the far left of the setup and pour all the grain in it. Place the small cup(s) in the bin on top of the grain. Set the second large bin on the floor at the far right of the setup.

3. Set the four graduated stands in a parallel line between the two large bins so that they get gradually lower from left to right (as the assembly views them).

4. Set the four small cartons on the four stands. Determine the proper spacing of the stands and the length of the tubing for the setup to work. Each carton needs to flow into the next.

5. Cut the four plastic or cardboard tubes to the desired length. Cut a hole in one side of each carton so that a tube will fit snugly into each hole. The placement of the holes is crucial to the proper flow of the grain so you may have to experiment (this is what the extra cartons are for). Our holes were placed about a third of the way up from the bottom of each carton.

6. Place a tube into the side of each carton and tape it securely in place from the inside with duct tape. Tape also helps smooth the opening and facilitate the flow of grain.

7. Set the cartons on their stands and adjust both stands and cartons so that the tube from each carton extends over the open top of the

carton on its right. The tube from the lowest carton will extend over the large bin on the right of the setup.

8. Test the setup by getting several people to scoop the grain, cup by cup, into the first carton on the left. This takes time now but prevents disaster later. Make sure that there is enough grain for each participant to share (the size of the scoop cup affects this) and that all the grain flows through the system and ends up in the bin on the right. Some grain will remain in each carton. Make needed adjustments to the setup and retest as necessary.

9. Label the bins with the pictures or symbols you have created. We labeled the large bin on the left with the outstretched hand bearing grain (facing right) and the large bin on the right with the empty outstretched hand (facing left). From left to right the four cartons were marked as follows: (1) a picture/symbol of home; (2) a picture/symbol of parish community; (3) a picture/symbol of America; (4) a picture/symbol of earth.

23. Sharing the Seed of God's Blessings: A Celebration of Thanksgiving

Outline of the Ritual

- Gathering Hymn (Any suitable thanksgiving hymn)
- Signing in Faith/Sign of the Cross
- Opening Prayer

    God, our Creator,
    gratitude fills our hearts as your blessings lie before us.
    We praise you as the bounty of your goodness overflows into our lives.
    Today we seek to share those gifts so that the poor and the hungry may also approach you with thankful hearts.
    We ask this through Christ, our Lord. Amen.

- 1st Reading (2 Cor 9:7–12: generosity produces thanks)
- Response (any setting of a thanksgiving psalm)
- Gospel Acclamation
- Gospel (Lk 12:16–21: parable of the rich fool)
- Homily
- Ritual Action (All process forward and offer canned goods. Each participant or family pours a small cup of seed into the first bin and returns to their places. Gradually these simple sharings overflow and produce thanksgiving. Music during ritual: Instrumental music or an antiphonal hymn may accompany this action; however, the sound of the flowing grain is integral to the sign and should remain part of the ritual experience.)
- Our Father
- Sign of Peace
- Blessing and Dismissal
- Closing Hymn ("Now Thank We All Our God," M. Rinkart and J. Cruger, traditional)

24. Let Our Prayer Rise Before You: A Rite of Intercession

This ritual of intercessory prayer can stand alone or be used as a more pronounced way of presenting the general intercessions at Eucharist. It is well suited for a special occasion or a time of particular need when there is a sense of greater solemnity or urgency about the community's prayer of intercession.

Preparation for the Service

- several vessels for burning charcoal and incense (Censers work if you have enough of them, but small ceramic bowls also work well. We purchased inexpensive small metal pots with removable lids at a kitchen supply store.)

- sand to place in each vessel for the charcoal to rest upon (We needed this because our makeshift censers got hot on the bottom. Depending on what you work with, sand may not be necessary.)

- a piece of charcoal for each burner

- incense, enough for each burner

- containers for incense, one for each burner (We suggest cups or small bowls.)

- a spoon for each incense container

1. Decide on how many prayer stations you need based upon how many people will engage in the ritual. You may invite everyone to come forward, or you may select community representatives to do so.

2. At each station place one of the burners, pour a base of sand in the bottom if needed, and place a piece of charcoal in it.

3. Set a container of incense next to each burner and place a spoon in each one.

4. Prior to the service, light the charcoal at each station. Make sure to do this five to ten minutes early to allow the charcoal to light thoroughly.

5. Instruct the assembly to place only a few grains of incense in each burner at a time; otherwise the charcoal gets smothered and the symbol is diminished.

Outline for the Ritual

- Gathering Hymn ("To You O Lord," Owen Alstott, OCP)
- Signing in Faith/Sign of the Cross
- Opening Prayer (for the blessing of human labor in the sacramentary)
- 1st Reading (1 Thes 5:16–24)
- Response (Ps 26; setting: "I Lift Up My Soul," Tim Manion, New Dawn)
- Gospel Acclamation
- Gospel (Mt 7:7–11)
- Homily
- Intercessions/Ritual Action (Note: If this rite is used in the context of a Eucharist, the incense ritual is inserted at the general intercessions. Members of the assembly or community representatives are invited forward to sprinkle a few grains of incense on a censer. As they do so, they may express petitions either silently or aloud. The procedure for this rite will depend in part upon the size of the assembly and the numbers engaged in the ritual. Hymn during ritual: "Let My Prayer Rise Before You," Paul Inwood, St. Thomas More Group. The antiphonal style of this hymn allows participation during the ritual; if petitions are voiced aloud, the song is sung afterward.)
- The Lord's Prayer
- Sign of Peace
- Blessing and Dismissal
- Closing Hymn (any appropriate hymn of your choice)

25. Many Yet One: A Celebration of Unity

This ritual is a way for pastoral staffs, faculties, or small communities to mark the beginning of a new year, a joint venture, or a workshop or institute. Its emphasis upon unity in diversity also makes it suitable as a reconciliation service for a community that has experienced tension or division. It can also provide an alternative to the "unity candle" ceremony used at many weddings. In fact, this rite first developed out of dissatisfaction with the unity candle as a fitting symbol of the union marriage signifies. The idea of the individual being extinguished upon entering a relationship seems inconsistent with developmental psychology and sacramental theology. As the joke goes: "Couples agree that 'the two should become one'; the problem starts when they try to decide which one."

We present this rite in a very simple form here; however, it may be expanded or used as a gathering rite or a prayer for unity in the context of a larger prayer experience. Feel free to adapt it for your needs.

Preparation for the Ritual

- a supply of rose petals in different colors, one for each participant. (Many florists sell rose petals separately.)
- two or more decorative dishes or platters for the petals
- one large glass bowl with a large circumference or surface area (Something similar to a punch bowl works well.)
- three stands on which to display the vessels
- drapings to place over the stands

1. Choose a central place for setting up the unity symbol.

2. Place the glass bowl on a stand at a focal point of the environment.

3. Place the two dishes on stands on either side of and slightly behind the bowl. Several dishes may surround the large bowl if you wish.

4. Divide the rose petals evenly and place them on the two dishes or divide them among several dishes, according to color.

5. Fill the glass bowl about two-thirds full of water.

Note: If you feel ambitious, you may wish to experiment with the setup which first inspired this service, something we saw at a family wedding years ago. Try fashioning a display of running water where water from two raised vessels would flow down separate channels into one common bowl. In this scenario, the participants would place blossoms or petals into one of the separate upper containers which would then be carried by the water down into the one large pond. We did not have the time or resources to get this to work to our satisfaction, but we believe it would make the symbol more effective if it could be done.

Outline for the Ritual

- Gathering Hymn ("Gather Us In," Marty Haugen, GIA)
- Signing in Faith/Sign of the Cross
- Greeting or Opening Prayer
- Penitential Rite (focused on the call to unity)
- 1st Reading (1 Cor 12:12–20)
- Response (any setting of Ps 133)
- Gospel Acclamation
- Gospel (Mt 14:13–20)
- Homily
- Ritual Action (Each member of the community processes forward, takes a rose petal from one of the individual dishes, and places it in the community pool. Hymn during ritual: "We Are Many Parts," Marty Haugen, GIA)
- Intercessions (prayers for unity and other appropriate petitions)
- The Lord's Prayer (Invite the community to join hands.)
- Sign of Peace
- Blessing and Dismissal
- Closing Hymn (any suitable hymn of unity or praise)

26. Salt of the Earth: A Rite of Ecological Justice

This ritual combines the concept of witness with an invitation to take responsibility for the environment. It uses the symbol of the earth, a rich symbol in creation-centered theology, to echo God's call that we live in harmony with the world. While the rite will certainly work exclusively as a celebration of witness, we recommend the environmental focus. We also suggest that the rite include a specific environmental action on the part of the community so that life action and ritual action remain partners. Some adaptation will make this service suitable for just about any age group, but we first used it with high school students. It is possible to celebrate this rite on its own or within the context of Eucharist. The size of the globe we constructed and describe below, however, makes for an imposing symbol and merits consideration of whether such a visually dominating sign will enhance or distract from the Eucharist.

Preparation for the Service

- a world globe (We had a large worship space, so we made a large globe. If you have a smaller environment or prefer a simpler approach, world globes of many sizes are readily available in schools, at teacher stores, and at "Rand-McNally" outlets. See instructions for making your own globe at the end of this section.)
- a stand or table for the globe
- a 26-ounce box of table salt
- three or four small glass dishes or bowls
- eight to twelve votive candles, matches, and a taper candle
- eight to twelve clear glass vigil light holders (Clear plastic cups will suffice.)
- a recording of "Land of Confusion" from the Genesis album *Invisible Touch* (We edited out the slow bridge section that seemed unrelated to our witness message.)
- slides to accompany the Genesis song, especially slides depicting witness, ministry, creative use of hands, and the earth (This is an option for those with interest and experience in this medium.)

To Make Your Own Globe

If you choose to make your own globe you need the following:

- a beach ball about four feet in diameter (available at most major toy stores)
- several cans of blue spray paint for oceans (Be sure to buy environmentally safe spray paint or avoid paint altogether by finding a solid blue beach ball.)
- a world atlas with continents proportionate to globe size
- lots of newspaper cut or torn into strips as for papier-maché
- a bottle of glue and a bowl of water as for papier-maché

1. Blow up the beach ball and seal the air nozzle with the plug, making sure that the seal is tight and there are no leaks.
2. Make papier-maché-like strips with the glue and newspaper strips. If you have a solid blue ball you may skip the papier-maché.
3. Cover the beach ball with two or three layers of papier-maché strips.
4. Allow the papier-maché shell to dry thoroughly overnight.
5. Spray the globe with the blue paint to form the oceans.
6. Allow the paint to dry thoroughly.
7. Cut out the continents from the atlas and glue or tape them onto the globe. An artist, if available, could paint continents by hand.

Note: Once the globe is finished it cannot be deflated. Be sure it will fit through any doors it needs to before making it.

8. Choose a prominent place for the globe in your environment and set it on its stand.
9. Place the unlighted vigil lights in a ring around the globe, far enough from the globe to avoid a fire hazard. Set matches and a taper candle nearby for lighting the candles.
10. Set three or four glass dishes in front of the globe.
11. Pour enough salt into each glass dish so that it will be visible to the assembly.

26. Salt of the Earth: A Rite of Ecological Justice

Outline for the Ritual

- Gathering Hymn ("Sing Out Earth and Skies," Marty Haugen, GIA)
- Signing in Faith/Sign of the Cross
- Opening Prayer
- 1st Reading (Is 60:1–4 or a Genesis creation account)
- Response (Ps 98; setting: "All the Ends of the Earth," Haugen/Haas, GIA)
- Gospel Acclamation
- Gospel (Mt 5:13–16)
- Homily (Focus on witness, the gift of creation, the ecological crisis, and stewardship.)
- Ritual Action (Each member of the assembly comes forward, takes a pinch of salt, and sprinkles it on the world globe as a commitment to give witness and/or care for the earth. After all have become "salt for the earth" selected representatives from the community light the ring of vigil candles around the globe. Lights are dimmed to highlight "the light of the world" from the candles and to prepare for the slide reflection. Hymn during action: "What You Hear in the Dark," Dan Schutte, New Dawn)
- Slide Reflection ("Land of Confusion": Project slides over the globe while lighted candles illuminate it.)
- Intercessions
- Blessing and Commissioning (All are sent forth to care for creation. These are best written by the community to reflect its own mission.)
- Closing Hymn (any suitable hymn of witness or creation)

27. Baptized in Water and the Spirit: A Prayer for Catechumens

We have used this ritual as part of a session for catechumens and candidates. We have usually incorporated it into the period of inquiry as a way of introducing the basic symbols of initiation and involving inquirers in praying with those symbols. This service also works with other groups such as adult education gatherings, "Renew" or Christ Renews His Parish groups, or parish prayer groups. It may also be suitable for groups facing internal tension or division because the ritual celebrates the reconciliation of opposites, the power of paradox, and the unity amid diversity, which are so deeply rooted in Gospel teachings. We have found that this service works best by dividing those gathered into a number of small groups.

Preparation for the Ritual

- a gathering space for small groups
- a table and chairs for each group
- two small, attractive glass dishes or bowls for each table
- a pitcher of water and a jar of olive oil (The oil may be scented if desired. Fill one of the glass dishes on each table half full of water; fill the other half full of oil. You will not need this much liquid, but a generous sign is more powerful.)
- several napkins for each table

Outline for the Ritual

- Signing in Faith/Sign of the Cross
- Opening Prayer (Focus on reconciliation through "water and the Spirit.")
- Reading (Jn 3:1–8: Jesus and Nicodemus)
- Reflection (Focus on the paradox of baptism, the power of opposites. Without getting into literal explanations, mention the paradoxical nature of water and oil, the fact that the basic symbols of initiation "don't mix" yet yield great power in the life of the Christian community.)

- Ritual Action (One leader at each table—ideally a member of the catechumenate team—stands and takes the dish of water. The leader instructs all participants to rest their right hands on the table with the palms facing up. The leader moves around the table and signs each person's right hand with the water in the form of a cross. Next the leader asks the participants to rest their left hands on the table with palms up. The leader moves around the table and signs each person's left hand with the oil in the form of a cross. When all have been signed with water and oil, the leader invites everyone to join hands around the table, uniting water and oil in each pair of hands. Leaders should use enough water and oil to make the sign effective.

- Prayer (While hands are joined, say the "Our Father" or other suitable prayer. After this prayer the napkins may be used to remove the oil and water.)

- Simple Blessing or Sign of Peace

28. I Will Plant a Seed: A Rite of Intercession

This is a rather simple ritual that we have used primarily within the context of a sophomore high school retreat day. Still, it has the depth and flexibility to serve a variety of situations or age groups. This ritual takes the simple action of planting a mustard seed and makes it into both a participative intercessory prayer and a public witness to the people and causes which the faith community cares about. Our retreat groups have celebrated this liturgy informally while gathered on a carpeted floor around the primary symbols. A more formal setting and environment would certainly work just as well. Please note that this service is best celebrated with a relatively small number of people since it is designed to invite each member of the assembly to engage in the prayer-action.

Preparation for the Ritual

- a supply of mustard seed, enough to fill a small glass vessel and be readily visible to the gathered assembly (You will find this at many health food stores.)

- a pitcher of water

- two glass dishes or vessels, one each for the seed and the water (Match their size to the worship space and location.)

- potting soil (available at a garden center) or planting soil from your own yard (There should be enough soil to fill whatever planting container you use.)

- a planting container for the soil ("Terra pot" saucers are sold at garden centers and nurseries for moderate prices and provide an "earthenware" look. Be sure to obtain a container that has sufficient planting space for the number of people in the assembly. Surface area is more important than depth here.)

1. Place the planter in the worship space so that it is central and visible to the assembly. Raise it up on a stand if necessary.

2. Fill the planter with the potting soil.

3. On one side of the planter set the glass vessel filled with mustard seed.

4. On the other side of the planter set the glass vessel filled with water.

5. You may display a Bible or lectionary if you wish.

Instructions for the Assembly

These instructions may be given before the service or after the reflection. Each person who comes forward is invited to engage in three simple actions:

1. Take one of the mustard seeds from the glass vessel and press it into the soil anywhere in the planter.

2. As the seed is being planted the person says aloud: "I will plant a seed for...," completing the statement with the name of a person or intention to be remembered, e.g., "my mother," "a successful surgery," "Julie," "preservation of the rain forests."

3. Dip two or three fingers into the water and shake some of it over the planted seed as a blessing and nurturing action. This action signifies the importance of our participation in the efficacy of our prayer.

The service will continue until all who wish to make an intention come forward. It is important that people come forward one at a time rather than in groups or lines. This allows for a reflective pace and for hearing and participating in one another's prayers.

Outline of the Ritual

Note: This is not a fully developed ritual because we have usually used it in the context of a retreat day. You may wish to expand this outline for your purposes.

- Gathering (The assembly gathers around the planter. A hymn or opening prayer is suitable here.)

- Reading (Lk 14:20–21: the parable of the mustard seed)

- Optional Reflection (Instructions can be given at this time.)

- Prayer Action (Assembly comes forward one at a time to plant prayer intentions.)

- Our Father (All join hands around the planter to nurture the planted intentions of the community with this or some other suitable closing prayer.)

- Sign of Peace

- Dismissal (A closing hymn may be sung here.)

28. I Will Plant a Seed: A Rite of Intercession

Note: If the assembly will meet again or will be in ongoing contact with one another, the planter may be maintained and placed in a visible location where the participants will see it and remember all the prayers that have been planted there. Members may also be assigned to water and tend to the plants so that all may witness the gradual growth of the seeds of prayer they have planted.

29. The Green and the Gold: A Rite of Balance

This ritual was used toward the end of a pastoral certificate program in which the students were preparing to move into some form of ministry. It celebrates the importance of balance in ministry; the green by which we renew ourselves and the gold by which we spend ourselves for others. The dual focus of this rite, then, was to send the program's graduates forth with a commitment to both generosity and personal renewal. The green and the gold were symbols which could call them to this essential balance in life and in ministry. This service was celebrated at that time of the year when the leaves were just beginning to change from summer greens to fall golds. Thus, nature's cycle of the seasons provided the model for the life truth which we were celebrating. Although this rite was first used at a time of leavetaking, it is not a leavetaking rite by nature. It can be celebrated at any time in a community's life when the value of balance needs to be celebrated or affirmed.

Preparation for the Ritual

- a large basket for leaves (or two matching baskets if you prefer)
- a collection of green or summer leaves, one for each participant
- a collection of gold or fall leaves, one for each participant
- extra leaves or garlands of leaves in both colors for setting the environment (Garlands of artificial leaves are available at craft stores. The amount of leaves will vary according to the size of the worship space.)
- a worship aid printed in two colors (Half the copies should be printed on green paper, the other half on gold paper.)

Note: A choice must be made between real leaves, which would be collected off the ground, and artificial leaves, which can be found in nurseries and craft stores. For environmental reasons we do not recommend picking leaves from trees before they have fallen. Real leaves are the preferred option, yet other factors inevitably come into play which require each planner to make this decision at his or her own discretion. One must consider the availability of suitable real leaves, the availability of sufficient numbers of leaves in both green and gold, and the longevity of the symbol beyond this ceremony. If you wish the participants to keep the symbol, artificial leaves may be preferable because they last longer. Real leaves could still be an option, however, if you press them in wax and mount them on cardboard. This would preserve them while providing an attractive means of display for the participants.

1. Place the basket(s) in a focal point of the worship space. We suggest setting the basket(s) on a stand of some kind.

2. Fill the basket with an equal mixture of green and gold leaves, making sure there is one of each kind for every participant. If you are using two baskets, place the green leaves in one and the gold leaves in the other. If you have preserved and mounted the leaves in sets, you may prefer to use a table instead of a basket on a stand.

3. Enhance the setting according to your needs and tastes. One suggestion is to drape garlands of green and gold leaves from the basket(s) down to the floor.

Outline for the Ritual

- Welcome/Greeting

- Signing in Faith/Sign of the Cross

- Opening Prayer ("An Autumn Psalm of Fearlessness," Edward Hayes, from *Prayers for a Planetary Pilgrim* [Forest of Peace Books]. We suggest that all recite this prayer in unison or alternate in antiphonal style.)

- 1st Reading (Dt 30:15–19)

- Response (Ps 23; setting: "Shepherd Me, O God," Marty Haugen, GIA)

- Gospel (Mk 8:34–36 or Lk 10:38–42)

- Homily (the balance of giving and receiving, "green and gold" in life and in ministry)

- Ritual Action (Participants process forward and take one of each leaf from the basket(s) or are presented with a mounted set of both leaves. We prefer the former option because this action better symbolizes the truth that we must choose this balance for ourselves. After they take the leaves they are directed to stand in a circle for the dismissal rites. Hymn during ritual: "What Shall I Give?" Scott

29. The Green and the Gold: A Rite of Balance

Soper, OCP. An option for music during this ritual is "The Circle of Life" from the soundtrack to *The Lion King*.)

- Sprinkling Rite (Participants hold their leaves and are affirmed in the cycle of renewal they began at baptism. Hymn during sprinkling: "Rain Down," Scott Soper, OCP)

- Closing Prayer ("The Green and the Gold," antiphonal style)

   All: Like trees of life,
   we spring from the seeds of generous oaks
   who have stood majestic before our time
   and taught us the wisdom of sturdy roots
   and the daring of reaching limbs.

   Side A: We mature in their shadow
   and long to see the open space above their branches
   even as we take comfort in the shadow of their care.

   Side B: Their leaves, green and full,
   shade us from the heat and nourish us into life,
   even as their leaves grow withered and golden
      in the giving,
   and even in falling to the ground
   offer us nourishment in their final breath.

   Side A: Now we are grown tall and strong
   and learn the way of all things:
   "Give back what you have been given."
   We offer the seeds of our lives
      to sprout future generations;
   we extend our branches over them
      to protect them as they grow.

   Side B: We strive for balance,
   to know the course of all things,
   to receive the goodness of others
   and to give that all may live.

   Side A: May we live the giving and the taking
   the rest and the work
   the letting go and the holding on
   the risk and the reward.

Side B: Give us your blessing,
God of all life,
that we may never be cursed for not giving
nor lifeless for not renewing ourselves.

All: Keep us ever full and balanced
in the green and the gold.

- Sign of Peace
- Farewell Blessing and Sending Forth
- Closing Hymn (optional)

30. Home and Family Rites

The following set of rituals is intended to help families experience sacred, sacramental moments at home in a natural, familial environment. These experiences can give them a better understanding of and appreciation for sacramental moments in the other dimensions of their lives.

Since the family unit is ideally the primary religious educator, these rituals are aimed at helping the families to be more festive and imaginative in prayer. They also focus on a moment out of time; all gathered together with the phone off the hook or the answering machine engaged and no interruptions allowed.

Because our symbols are rooted in story, each ritual begins with Scripture. Each also includes time for sharing, for action, and for response. An important thing to remember is that they should not be rushed. We are not trying to teach; we are attempting to evoke a response. The focus of the prayer is not vertical, from us up to God, but horizontal, from one of us to another.

The goal of these rites is to show through symbols and moments that each person is important, each person is valuable and lovable. No one is alone because we are all sacraments to one another. The prayer leader can be any family member or guest who is chosen or gifted to serve in that capacity: parent, child, friend, relative, etc. The prayer services that follow focus on these basic Christian symbols: cross, washing of feet, sharing of bread, oil, word, laying on hands, fire, and water.

Preparations for Each Service

All should gather in a small area, near one another. Either sit around a table, on the floor, or on chairs—whatever is natural and comfortable. One person reads the Scripture, or several read in parts.

Cross

Scripture: Mk 8:34–38

Sharing: After a brief quiet reflection, discuss the reading using any of the following:
- Name some of the crosses we carry.
- Do we fight them or willingly, joyfully accept them?

- Do we see our crosses as a bond we share with Jesus and with all people?
- Do we see others' crosses? Do we look?
- How did Simon feel about carrying Jesus' cross? Did he accept it or say, "That's his problem, not mine."
- Does this reading relate to a recent experience?

Action:
1. Each person makes a small cross from available wooden materials (twigs, popsicle sticks, plywood, etc.). Don't rush; play quiet music on the stereo.
2. Read Lk 23:26.
3. Carry your cross with you the next day; let it remind you of your struggle; let it strengthen you.
4. The following days the family exchanges crosses and each member carries someone else's cross during that day. Let this action be a means of being present to their struggle.
5. Continue exchanging crosses daily until everyone has carried each family member's cross for one day.

Washing of Feet

Note: There is value in experiencing the awkwardness of washing feet. That was one of the points Jesus was making with this action. However, if this awkwardness gets in the way of the prayer experience, you may choose to wash each other's hands instead.

Scripture: Jn 13:1,3–17

Sharing: After a brief quiet reflection, discuss the reading, using any of the following:
- What did the reading say to you?
- What does it mean?
- What did you like best? What did you like least?
- Whom did you identify with in the story? Why?
- Why did they wash feet in Jesus' time?

- How do we welcome someone into our home?
- How do we welcome people into the church using water?
- What services do we do for each other that resemble the washing of feet in their awkwardness and difficulty?
- How do you feel when you are served? How do you feel when you are the server? Who gains? Why?

Action:
1. Each person washes another person's feet.
2. Read Matthew 25:31–40.

Oil

Note: For this ritual you will need some scented olive oil and some paper and pencil for each participant.

Scripture: Mt 26:6–10

Action:

1. Have each person make a list of their best traits (no negatives allowed!). Some people may need more time than others. We are all so busy looking for our faults we forget our virtues. We are loved and beautiful in God's eyes. These things are what God sees in you.

2. Go around the circle, focusing in turn on each individual. Family members then identify their favorite qualities in the person being focused upon.

3. After each member speaks, he or she traces a cross with oil on the forehead of the designated individual. Proceed until all family members are signed.

4. Pray Ps 133, together if possible.

Bread and Wine

Note: In today's fast-paced, overly busy culture, it is becoming rare for a family to sit down to dinner together. For this ritual, plan to leisurely prepare and share a meal together. What you eat is not important. It can be your family's favorite meal, something simple or complicated. What is important is that you prepare (cook, set the table, clean up, etc.) together and eat leisurely together. Sit around a table; use the good dishes and candlelight. This is a special evening.

Scripture: Mt 26:26–30

Action:

1. Leader takes a piece of bread, breaks off a piece, and invites all to do so.

2. The leader takes a drink from the cup of wine (juice) and invites all to do so.

3. Read Mt 15:32–38.

4. Eat dinner, taking lots of time for conversation, storytelling, etc. Enjoy each other's company. Conversation might include a discussion of how such special family meals are a continuation and a lead-in to Sunday Eucharist.

5. Read Acts 2:42–47.

6. When the meal is over, all clean up together. This should inspire a response!

Word

Scripture: Lk 24:13–35

Sharing: After a brief quiet reflection, discuss the reading, using any of the following.

- What is your favorite Scripture story? Why?

- What is your favorite family story? Why?

- How do we listen to the readings at church? Do we hear them? Do we listen carefully? Do we understand them as stories?

- Imagine you are a Christian in the early church. How excited would you be to hear the stories from the disciples, the first witnesses to Jesus? Imagine yourselves gathered to listen to letters from Paul and Peter.

Action:

1. Get out the family photo album and choose favorite pictures that reflect family, community, or church development.

2. Tell the stories behind the pictures.

Laying On of Hands

Scripture: Mt 19:13–15

Sharing: After a brief quiet reflection, discuss the reading, using any of the following:

- Do we celebrate our sicknesses, weaknesses, our reconciliations, our seeking wholeness, our need of human touch?
- When times are hard, do we gather close together to hold and help and support one another?
- If two members of a family have a conflict, the whole family suffers. Can the entire family help the healing process?

Action:

1. Examine the way you and any person present may have hurt one another by word, deed, or omission.

2. Be reconciled by talking with that person about how to resolve the hurt.

3. Lay your hands on that person's head as a sign of forgiveness or simply hug one another.

4. Read Mk 16:17–18.

Fire

Note: For this service you will need one large tabletop candle and a small taper or votive candle for each family member. Gather everyone in a dark place around the large burning candle. Each person has his/her small unlighted candle in front of them.

Scripture: Jn 12:35–36

Sharing: After a brief quiet reflection all should discuss the following question: "In what concrete, practical ways can we be a light for each other and for the world?"

Action:

1. As each person identifies his/her way of being a light, that person's candle is lighted from the center candle.

2. Read Mt 5:14–16.

Water

Note: For this service you will need a small but attractive vessel, such as a glass bowl, filled with water. Place the vessel of water in the middle of the table where you meet.

Scripture: Jn 3:1–5

Sharing: After a brief quiet time for reflection, talk about the many ways that water is vital, life-giving, refreshing, and fun (everything from crying tears to running through a lawn sprinkler).

Action:
1. All members of the group extend their hands over the water and ask God's blessing on the water with these or similar words: Lord, bless this water, a sign of our life in you.
2. Each member of the group signs the person next to him/her with the water. The water can be poured, sprinkled, or traced on the forehead.

More Liturgical Resources

LEADING THE ASSEMBLY IN PRAYER
A Practical Guide for Lay and Ordained Presiders
Michael J. Begolly

Paper, 160 pages, 5.5" x 8.5", ISBN: 0-89390-398-1

Priesthood is a gift of baptism, and, when ordained ministers are in short supply, other members of the community need to be ready to lead prayer. Michael J. Begolly shows you how to develop the skills and background you need to be a competent, prayerful worship leader. Great for both lay and ordained leaders.

MODERN LITURGY ANSWERS THE 101 MOST-ASKED QUESTIONS ABOUT LITURGY
Nick Wagner

Paper, 144 pages, 5.5" x 8.5", ISBN: 0-89390-369-8

Everyone has a question about liturgy. Get answers from the editor of MODERN LITURGY magazine. You'll learn the historical and theological background of current liturgical practices and you'll get practical solutions to vexing pastoral problems. Use this important reference book for your planning or just to provide quick authoritative answers.

THE WORD AND EUCHARIST HANDBOOK
Lawrence J. Johnson

Paper, 168 pages, 6" x 9", ISBN: 0-89390-276-4

The Word and Eucharist Handbook is your complete reference guide to liturgy. Designed for worship planners, ministers, and liturgical artists, it answers your questions about the origin, development, and modern practice of each part of the Mass.

Call Toll-Free 1-888-273-7782 for current prices.
See last page for ordering information.

Music and Celebrations

CELEBRATING THE EARTH
An Earth-Centered Theology of Worship with Blessings, Prayers, and Rituals
Scott McCarthy
Paper, 350 pages, 5.5" x 8.5", ISBN: 0-89390-199-7

Find out how an authentic Christian spirituality honors the rhythm of the seasons, the natural cycle of death and rebirth, and indigenous plant and animal life. The 26 blessings, prayers, and rituals reveal the beauty and balance found in creation. Works great in ecumenical settings.

COME, LET US CELEBRATE!
Creative Reconciliation Services
Robert Eimer, OMI, & Sarah O'Malley, OSB
Paper, 87 pages, 7" x 10", ISBN: 0-89390-082-6

These sixteen communal reconciliation services are adaptable for Rites II and III of the Roman Catholic sacrament of penance. They have been used in a parish setting and are easy to re-create. Each has symbols and themes carried out in the prayers, homily, examination, scripture readings, and songs.

EVALUATING YOUR LITURGICAL MUSIC MINISTRY
Keith L. Patterson
Paper, 160 pages, 8.5" x 11", ISBN: 0-89390-258-6

If you are interested in finding out how effective your church's liturgical music program is, this workbook will help you with your evaluation. The author includes all the information you need for surveying and measuring the quality and effectiveness of your present liturgical music, then guides you in implementing the changes necessary to improve your church's worship experience.

Call Toll-Free 1-888-273-7782 for current prices.
See last page for ordering information.

Resources for your Small Group

WHY SMALL CHRISTIAN COMMUNITIES WORK
Msgr. Timothy O'Brien with Margaret Gunnell
Paper, 64 pages, 5.5" x 8.5", ISBN: 0-89390-371-X

The key to forming Christians is forming small communities. In a small Christian community, says Msgr. Timothy O'Brien, you cannot be anonymous. You have to share your faith and relate to others. And to be in communities with Jesus is to experience the God's unconditional love of everyone. Great for all newly formed faith-sharing groups or anyone contemplating forming such a group. Bulk prices available.

LORD YOU MUST BE JOKING
Bible Stories That Tell Your Story
Eugene Webb

Paper, 176 pages, 5.5" x 8.5", ISBN: 0-89390-309-4
Leaders Guide: Paper, 80 pages, 5.5" x 8.5", ISBN: 0-89390-310-8

Here are stories set into a biblical context with a twist that makes you think. Reflection questions help the process. Use the leaders guide for retreats or other group situations.

GOOD NEWS FOR YOUR AUTUMN YEARS
Reflections on the Gospel of Luke
T. Josephine Lawler, OP

Paper, 144 pages, 6" x 9", ISBN: 0-89390-303-5
Leader's Guide: Paper, 48 pages, 6" x 9", ISBN: 0-89390-305-1

Good News for Your Autumn Years takes the special spirituality of the older adult into account. Sr. T. Josephine Lawler, a specialist on aging, notes how Luke's gospel parallels the life cycle of human beings. Large type and gentle reflection questions make this a friendly book. With the help of a leader's guide, you can use this book as the basis for five faith-sharing sessions.

Call Toll-Free 1-888-273-7782 for current prices.
See last page for ordering information.

Stories for Faith-Sharing

STORIES TO INVITE FAITH-SHARING
Experiencing the Lord Through the Seasons
Mary McEntee McGill
Paper, 128 pages, 5.5" x 8.5", ISBN: 0-89390-230-6

Sharing our stories makes our faith journey easier. These twenty stories are based on real life experiences which help us recognize God's presence in everyday life. Reflections and questions for group sharing can lead to personal awareness and prayer. Great for faith-sharing groups, workshops, and retreats.

DEEPDOWN SPIRITUALITY
Seasonal Stories That Invite Faith-Sharing
Joseph J. Juknialis
Paper, 144 pages, 5.5" x 8.5", ISBN: 0-89390-392-2

Joseph J. Juknialis, a popular and imaginative storyteller, has turned his hand to real-life personal stories that work especially well for faith-sharing groups. This is a collection of poetic/prose reflections on the Sunday Scriptures throughout the three cycles of the lectionary. Topical and seasonal indices help you select the right story for the right time.

Call Toll-Free 1-888-273-7782 for current prices.
See last page for ordering information.

Catechize with Bulletin Inserts

MODERN LITURGY's Bulletin Inserts
Paul Turner
Perfectbound plus 3.5" HD diskette, 96 pages, 8" x 11", ISBN: 0-89390-414-7

Inserts in Sunday bulletins are an excellent way to gently and effectively catechize parishioners on liturgical subjects, but sometimes it can be difficult to prepare these inserts. MODERN LITURGY's Bulletin Inserts takes the hassle out of the preparation. These 80 bulletin inserts come complete and ready to use on diskette. All you need to do is electronically insert them into your parish bulletin. No retyping. No scanning of artwork. Your job is made much easier. If you create your bulletin without a computer, you can still use these inserts because the book includes camera-ready artwork which has already been laid out for you. Photocopying permission is included with all the inserts.

Paul Turner has been writing for MODERN LITURGY magazine for 6 years. He is pastor of St. John Regis Parish in Kansas City, MO and holds a doctorate in sacramental theology from Sant' Anselmo University in Rome.

Order from your local bookseller, or contact:

Resource Publications, Inc.
160 E. Virginia Street #290
San Jose, CA 95112-5876
1-408-286-8505 (questions)
1-408-287-8748 (fax)
1-888-273-7782 (orders, toll-free)
info@rpinet.com
www.rpinet.com